First Fruits Press
The Academic Open Press of Asbury Theological Seminary
859-858-2236
first.fruits@asburyseminary.edu
http://place.asburyseminary.edu/firstfruits

Asbury Theological Seminary
204 N. Lexington Ave., Wilmore, KY 40390
asburyseminary.edu
800-2ASBURY

The Autobiography of Bishop H.C. Morrison

Revised and Edited by
George H. Means

First Fruits Press
Wilmore, Kentucky
c2014

The Autobiography of Bishop H.C. Morrison, revised edited by George H. Means
Published by First Fruits Press, © 2014
Publishing House of the M.E. Church, South, © 1917

Digital version at http://place.asburyseminary.edu/firstfruitsheritagematerial/77/

First Fruits Press is a digital imprint of the Asbury Theological Seminary, B.L. Fisher Library. Asbury Theological Seminary is the legal owner of the material previously published by the Pentecostal Publishing Co. and reserves the right to release new editions of this material as well as new material produced by Asbury Theological Seminary. Its publications are available for noncommercial and educational uses, such as research, teaching and private study. First Fruits Press has licensed the digital version of this work under the Creative Commons Attribution Noncommercial 3.0 United States License. To view a copy of this license, visit http://creativecommons.org/licenses/by-nc/3.0/us/.

For all other uses, contact First Fruits Press:
859-858-2236
first.fruits@asburyseminary.edu

ISBN: 9781621711476 (print), 9781621711483 (digital)

Morrison, H. C. (Henry Clay), 1842-1921.
   The Autobiography of Bishop H.C. Morrison / revised and edited by George H. Means.
   256 p. : port. ; 21 cm.
   Wilmore, Ky. : First Fruits Press, c2014.
   Reprint. Previously published: Autobiography of Bishop Henry Clay Morrison. Nashville, Tenn. : Pub. House of the M.E. Church, South, c1917.
   ISBN: 9781621711476 (pbk.)
   1. Morrison, Henry Clay, 1842-1921. 2. Methodist Episcopal Church, South – Bishops -- Biography I. Title. II. Means, George H.
BX8495.M6 A2 2014   287.09

Cover design by Jane Brannen

BISHOP H. C. MORRISON

AUTOBIOGRAPHY

OF

Bishop Henry Clay Morrison

REVISED AND EDITED BY
GEORGE H. MEANS, D.D.

This above all: to thine own self be true,
And it must follow, as the night the day,
Thou canst not then be false to any man.
—Shakespeare.

NASHVILLE, TENN.
PUBLISHING HOUSE OF THE M. E. CHURCH, SOUTH
1917

Dedication

TO MY DEVOTED WIFE

Who has shared my labors for half a century and who has been my severest critic, and therefore the greatest help in my ministry, this volume is affectionately inscribed

CONTENTS.

	Page.
INTRODUCTION	7

CHAPTER I.
Ancestry and Youth.................................... 9

CHAPTER II.
Conversion 14

CHAPTER III.
The Ministry 20

CHAPTER IV.
Army Life 24

CHAPTER V.
Peace and Its Fruitage................................. 29

CHAPTER VI.
Marriage and Home Life................................ 40

CHAPTER VII.
City Life 47

CHAPTER VIII.
Connectional Duties 61

CHAPTER IX.
The Episcopacy 65

CONCLUSION BY THE EDITOR.............................. 80

APPENDIX.
Reminiscences and Reflections.......................... 87
Gospel Talks 101

INTRODUCTION.

PETER HORRY, the biographer and bosom friend of Francis Marion, exclaims: "O that my pen were a quill of the swan, that sings for future days! Then wouldst thou, my friend, receive the full measure of thy fame." This emotional expression of appreciation illustrates the real test of worth, the fame of future days, when all the facts are weighed in the balance of justice, when men are not swayed by friendship or warped prejudice, and when the world is converted to an impartial jury. Then, and not until then, can we measure the true worth of a faithful servant.

A biographer is too often prone to "lift a mortal to the skies or draw an angel down." And if the editor of this book had written a biography instead of editing an autobiography, no doubt he would have "dipped his pen in his heart," painted pictures in colors too gorgeous, and blurred the record by extravagant statements. As it is, we have the simple story of an active life, written without ostentation and without self-laudation, its life lessons glowing on every page for the good of rising generations and those that are yet to come.

The subject of this sketch has acted his part in many stormy periods of the Church that tried men's souls. By many he has been loved and revered, by some misunderstood; and it is expected that he should say something in justification of his conduct in certain vital emergencies, and he presents his case without rancor, simply letting the facts, as he understands them, speak for themselves.

Autobiography of Bishop Henry Clay Morrison.

Biographies and autobiographies are not measured by the same standard of appreciation. Friends esteem them because they perpetuate the memory of those they love, enemies question their truthfulness and treat them as a target for abuse, strangers value them for the useful facts and incidents they contain, and the great mass of readers neither know nor care about the conditions that controlled or the motives that actuated the man whose record they peruse as carelessly as they would scan the pages of a summer romance.

A jury is better fitted to render a verdict concerning an act when it knows the motives which actuated the actor. A vessel is often controlled by undercurrents which to the untutored mariner are unknown and unsuspected. There are emergencies arising in life which call for measures seemingly severe, and circumstances at other times demand a policy that may appear tame and unduly tolerant. Time only can unfold the real facts when the passing years have dulled the edge of unjust criticism.

"We can reason but from what we know." Courage is often attributed to rashness, and earnest importunity to a lack of discretion. In all life there are influences that impel a course of conduct contrary to the wishes of others, and yet which duty prompts us to pursue even when it conflicts with our own interests.

> "We live in deeds, not years; in thoughts, not breaths;
> In feelings, not in figures on a dial.
> We should count time by heart throbs. He most lives
> Who thinks most, feels the noblest, acts the best."
>
> THE EDITOR.

CHAPTER I.

ANCESTRY AND YOUTH.

> Our early days, how often back
> We turn on life's bewildering track,
> Where over hill and valley plays
> The sunlight of our early days! —*Gallagher.*

SCOTLAND was the home of my paternal ancestors, and the name is not unknown to history. From Scotland they came to North Carolina, and from there to my native State of Tennessee.

Andrew Wells was one of the settlers of French Lick, where the city of Nashville now stands. His two daughters were Nancy and Elizabeth. Elizabeth became the wife of Judge William Fitzgerald, of Paris, Tenn. He was at one time a member of the United States Congress. Nancy was married to Josiah Morrison, and their eldest son, Robert, was my father.

My maternal grandfather was Capt. Colmore Duvall, a native of Virginia. He married a lady from Maryland. His vocation was that of a contractor and builder, an "old Virginia gentleman" with some means. Coming West about the year 1800, he settled in Clarksville, the county seat of Montgomery County, Tenn., where he built the first courthouse in that town. By reason of broad hospitality and high life in the West, he soon found his little fortune consumed and soon after died, leaving my grandmother with no possessions save seven small children. But she was no ordinary woman. Her strong common sense, energy, and faith in God enabled her to meet the situation, and she reared her children, giving them the common-school education of that time. One of the sons died in childhood; the other received the benefit of a higher education. He bore his father's given name and was prominent as a teacher of languages. His son, Pitt Duvall, is now a presiding elder in the Louisville Conference.

My mother, Mary Duvall, was the third eldest of the five daughters. She and my father were married in 1834. He followed farming in his native State until 1857, when he removed to Graves County, in Western Kentucky, and later to the city of Paducah, where he closed his life at the age of seventy-seven years.

There were ten of us children; six have passed to the other life. One brother and two sisters remain. All are members of the Methodist Episcopal Church, South. C. W. Morrison was a lay member of the General Conference in 1902.

I first saw the light of this world on the 30th day of May, 1842, in a small, plain cottage about five miles from Clarksville, Tenn. Nature kindly gave me a strong physical constitution. I had perfect health, with a fine flow of spirits, and was seldom distanced or outdone in any childish sports. My mother was never solicitous lest I should prove one of those angelic children who are popularly supposed to be too good to remain in this world; she had no fear of my early death from this cause.

There are some incidents clear to my memory which

occurred before I was three years old. Here I shall record an incident greatly creditable to my father, though not complimentary to myself. I developed early, as many children do, a propensity for telling falsehoods. My father was a man of few words, but was a close observer of the moral trend and development of his children. Detecting this ruinous perversity in my nature, he proceeded at once to eliminate it. Finding that moral suasion was not effective, he resorted to Solomon's remedy, and a dozen or more sound evangelical thrashings wrought a complete cure; and but for my father's prompt and faithful dealing I might have grown up a common liar.

I record this as a note of warning to any overindulgent parents who may neglect their children's evil tendencies under the delusion that "they will get better as they grow older." "The child is father of the man," says the old proverb; and ignoring its wisdom, more than any other one thing, has filled our prisons with the fruitage of early crime.

As a consequence of my father's watchful care I soon learned perfect obedience to his will and words, and this held good with me from infancy to manhood. I now speak from a life of long observation, and I admonish parents to begin the control of their children before the little ones can talk or walk. Let them be your companions and be made to feel that you would die for them if need be, but inspire them with such reverence that they would almost rather die than disobey your command.

My parents were in quite moderate circumstances and unable to give me the opportunities they desired;

but they took pains to instill right principles into my child mind and prayed for me daily at the family altar.

My mother came of a literary family and was a constant reader of the best books to be had in that day, and she inspired me at an early age with an intense desire to obtain knowledge and an education. But the family was large. My sisters were to be sent to school. I was my father's only help in cultivating the farm, and I saw that I must husband my time and save the odd hours. So I became a student when a child, and the habit abides. I read the simple primers at five and was regarded as a good reader for a child at the age of six years.

I had the good fortune at the age of twelve years to get the benefit of eight months' instruction in a country school under a thoroughly capable teacher, John Kime, who afterwards married my eldest sister. He was rather an austere personage, a man of unquestioned integrity, and a consistent Christian. I had the benefit of his instruction at a time when I needed it most, when he became a member of our family, and his influence on my character was only second to that of my father.

During the aforementioned school term I was occasionally kept at home to help in the farm work. This, of course, threw me to the foot of my classes, though I would soon regain my place at their head. The teacher made a standing offer of a handsome reward to the pupil who would hold for ten days the head of the large spelling class. When, because of enforced absence, I had to take my place at the foot, he never had to award the prize.

Autobiography of Bishop Henry Clay Morrison.

I have ever held as the proudest hour of my life an incident in this school. I give it for the benefit of the boys who read this book. We had the old-time "spelling match," in which the school was divided into two equal companies. The two leaders would stand side by side and spell until one of them missed a word and was spelled down. Then came the next in line to take the place of the one who had fallen. On this occasion two young men had come from a neighboring school to challenge our school for a "spelling bee." I was one of the leaders that afternoon. My antagonist soon went down at my side, and so with the others that followed, until all had fallen, and I stood alone.

The two visitors were greatly elated at my triumph. The teacher then said: "Would you like to try the lad?" As they were there with a challenge, they could not well refuse. So the first, with evident embarrassment, arose and took his place at my side. He was at least twenty years of age and I a barefooted urchin—a picture of life's inequalities. But after a few words were given out the older contestant went down. His companion was at least six feet tall, and reluctantly he came to his place. He was tall enough to reach up and grasp the round pole that served as a joist. He grasped the pole and steadied himself for the ordeal. But the giant, like his companion, soon surrendered his sword. And as I looked upon the ranks on the opposite side, with their defeated champions, I felt a complacency I have never known since that memorable Friday afternoon in the little log schoolhouse.

CHAPTER II.

CONVERSION.

We heeded not the roaring blast, nor winter's icy air;
We found our climate in the heart, and it was summer there.
—*Drake.*

THE most momentous event in my boyhood or in my life was my conversion. My parents were Methodists, and my father's house was a home for Methodist preachers. And "there were giants in those days" in the Tennessee Conference. The names of Erwin, Green, Hughes, and Pitts were household words in Methodist homes.

The old-time camp meeting was in vogue. The tents were pitched in a hollow square, with the tabernacle, or preaching place, in the center. Rude seats for the auditors and plenty of clean wheat straw at the altar where the penitents knelt, a rustic platform for a pulpit, and a huge ox horn hung up in a convenient place to call the people to worship—this was the outfit. Thus equipped, the "sons of thunder" did such preaching as is seldom heard at this later and more scientific period. Such preaching was never more needed than now. Under such appeals the audiences were mightily moved, and multitudes cried for mercy and were saved.

Baker's Camp Ground, in Montgomery County, was situated on a beautiful, clear little creek bearing that name, about fourteen miles east of Clarksville, the county seat.

Rev. B. F. White was in charge of the annual camp

meeting in progress during August, 1856. I was then a lad of fourteen years and a penitent at that altar day and night.

My cousins, comrades, and neighbor boys were nearly all happily converted; but my way seemed dark and more and more hopeless until I was on the verge of despair. But suddenly the light broke upon me in my wretchedness, and I realized that I was saved. This wonderful deliverance came at about nine o'clock Wednesday night, August 6, 1856, and was an epoch which changed the whole tenor of my life, and of its genuineness and supernatural character I have never had a doubt. The transformation amazed me. The faces of the people, the encampment, the little stream, and the whole face of nature appeared to me as clothed with unearthly beauty, and this ecstatic state continued for weeks.

I record an incident which occurred under this abiding baptism. My mother was not with me at the camp meeting, but had heard of my conversion. Returning home at night, I rode to the barn to feed my horse. While drawing water from the old well among the mulberry trees a familiar hymn broke clearly upon my ears. I stood with my hand on the windlass and listened. It was the clear, sweet tones of my mother's voice singing an old song familiar at the camp meeting. The song ended, I finished my work and hastened to meet my mother. She met me quietly, pressed me to her heart, and "thanked God for her boy's happy conversion." But there had been no song. How was this? I could not understand it. It was so distinct, so natural, but it was all subjective. It was my own transformed spirit hearing with its newborn powers the voice and the song so often heard before.

I have ever been grateful to God for a clear, unquestioned, instantaneous conversion. There are two facts in life of which I have never had a doubt—my conversion and my call to the ministry. These two facts have been my stay in the close places and trying experiences of life. Under some pressures I might have given up to discouragement, but these two props which God placed under me have never been shaken.

I was received into the Church on probation the night before my conversion, but I was desperately in earnest to be saved. I doubt the wisdom of receiving into the Church persons who are not genuinely in earnest about their salvation. I believe the multitudes of unconverted and impenitent persons who have been taken—in many instances dragooned—into the Church have been no small hurt to our Zion. They derive no benefit from such a formal relation and only serve to illustrate the fact that "no man can serve two masters." To lead a new life one must be renewed by the Spirit of God, made a new creature.

I was received on probation and have never been received into full membership in the Church. I am still on trial. However, my name was retained on the Church roll. The "six months' probation" law was annulled. I have reckoned myself a Church member for sixty years, and the Church has borne with me as such.

A short time after my conversion there was an abatement of that "joy inexpressible," and I became fearful that I had lost the divine favor. But by reading the Scriptures I found that my fears were groundless; that I was saved by faith and not by feeling. And finding my faith in Christ the same, I now learned to trust him without the glow of spiritual joy as when its ecstasies filled my soul. And here I wish to quote a happy and helpful thought from "The Christian's Secret of a Happy Life": "When a doubt arises, remember from whence it comes. God will never put a doubt in the mind of his child. Then when a doubt comes you know it is from Satan and not from God. Hence you know at once what to do with it. Banish it to its own place."

In the autumn of 1857 my father moved from Tennessee and settled near Mayfield, in Graves County, Western Kentucky. Up to this time I had known nothing but buoyant health; but the new climate was to me unfriendly, and I soon went down with a malignant fever. And when the crisis came I overheard the old family physician tell my father that I would probably live six hours. I was not greatly alarmed; but I had an intense desire to live, and, like Hezekiah, "I turned my face to the wall" and carried the case to God. I pledged him that "if he would raise me up and let me live, whatever of life he granted me I would give to his service." He heard my plea and has added more than three times what he granted to the king.

My death was considered so certain that letters of condolence came to my parents and were generally full of eulogies of the departed. When the weary months had worn away and my good mother thought me strong enough to admit of it, she allowed me to read those letters. They were to me a revelation. It seemed that they must have referred to some one else; as touching myself, the half could not be true. To the surprise of every one, I came slowly back to life and strength. It was a weary process. Five long months' confinement to my room! The trees were yet green when I was stricken in the autumn, and the new leaves were budding when I walked out for the first time in the following spring. I had lived an age in that five months and came through a changed and chastened spirit. This was my first illness, and in it I learned how good it is to let God have his own way. And in after years I understood how he was educating me then to sympathize with suffering and to comfort the untold numbers of the afflicted who were to come under my pastoral care.

This long and almost fatal illness so undermined and weakened a naturally strong constitution that I was well-nigh an invalid for years afterwards, much of the time unable to leave my room, sometimes endeavoring to do light work on the farm, but through all the weary months pressing my studies to the extremity of my strength.

An incident here may encourage the young to seek to bring others to Christ. A youth of my acquaintance, though not my associate, was critically ill, with little hope of recovery. He lived perhaps three miles from my home. His parents were fatalists, and the poor lad had little knowledge of spiritual things. When out on the farm one afternoon that boy and his sad condition came to my mind in a strange and remarkable way, unlike anything in my experience. I tried in vain to throw off the impression and positively suffered under it. I appealed to my father and asked him to go and talk to the young man, but he declined. The load grew heavier, and at last I took the matter to my mother, and she sympathized with me in my dilemma.

A boy can always tell out his heart to his mother. When the evening meal was over, I mounted my horse in the moonlight and started over to talk to Tom about his soul. I had no experience in such work, had never tried to lead in public prayer, but now was strangely impelled to this undertaking. The good Hand was guiding; and although I met with a rebuff from his father, his mother sympathized, and I pressed the case. I explained the plan of salvation, of which he was utterly ignorant, and prayed with him from time to time when I visited him; and about my fourth visit I found that God had been there in the meantime, and the young man was gloriously saved.

The following evening, accompanied by my sister and the daughter of a Baptist neighbor, I visited the new convert and sang for him some hymns, which he greatly enjoyed. Returning, we left our neighbor friend at her home. That night at midnight she arose and went to her mother's room, happily converted and praising God.

About two weeks later God called the young man to come up higher. I was at his bedside when he passed to the other life in perfect peace. I expect to strike hands with Tom W—— among the first in our Father's house above. His was the first soul I ever won for Christ, before I had any thought of the ministry.

CHAPTER III.

THE MINISTRY.

> Wouldst thou from sorrow find a sweet relief,
>   Or is thy heart oppressed with woe untold?
> Balm wouldst thou gather for corroding grief?
>   Pour blessings round thee like a shower of gold.
> —*Wilcox.*

HAVING somewhat improved in health, though without strength to do farm work, I went before the school commissioners of the county, passed an examination, and was granted license to teach a common English school. This vocation I followed successfully for two years and greatly enjoyed it. I had not thought of it as my life work; indeed, I had not determined this matter of a vocation, which is so important to every young man.

I was walking to and fro one afternoon in the schoolroom, as was my habit, when instantly the impression came to me that it was my duty to preach the gospel. The impression was so sudden and forceful that I was completely consumed by it. I have no recollection of what occurred in the further work of that day. But this impression never left me. I tried every possible way to free myself from it. I thought I had many good excuses—poor health, inadequate preparation, and no experience before public assemblies. But the impression held me and continued with me for months before I made it known to my parents. They sympathized with me and prayed that God would guide me, but wisely feared to urge me too hastily to accept the call.

I believe that parents make a sad mistake when to any extent they take the responsibility of calling their sons to preach the gospel. They should only pray that if God calls they shall listen and obey. They are to do the encouraging only after God does the calling.

When I made my state of mind known to my parents, my mother then told me what she had never intimated to me before, that she had given me to God at my birth and that she had been praying all my life that God would call me into the ministry. This was a revelation to me and made such a profound impression that I made a full and final surrender of myself to the work to which God had called me.

My health was such that two eminent physicians assured me that I could not live twelve months if I went into the ministry. But I knew my duty and was willing to take the consequences. "I conferred not with flesh and blood."

I was licensed to preach on the fourth day of April, 1863, at Pleasant Hill Church, in Ballard County, Ky. I began at once trying to exercise my gifts. And while I am sure that it was more exhortation than preaching, yet God honored my poor efforts, the people heard, and numbers were converted.

I taught for one session after being authorized to preach, and God greatly blessed me in that work. The school was large, and many of the pupils were grown. The Holy Spirit was in touch with the school, and about twenty of the older scholars were converted in the schoolroom.

Autobiography of Bishop Henry Clay Morrison.

The Civil War was raging at this time, and most of my associates had gone to the field. I was physically unfit for service, insomuch that neither Federals nor Confederates paid me any attention, but left me to go unmolested to my appointments on the Sabbath day.

Western Kentucky lies in the bounds of the Memphis Conference, which was completely disorganized for the time by the war. Rev. Finley Bynum, then prominent in the Conference, wrote me urging me to take the place of junior preacher with Rev. J. M. Flatt, then pastor of the Clinton Circuit. Responding to this call, my first home-leaving was almost a tragedy. Mayfield Creek was dangerous; it was deep, and its banks were precipitous. This stream I had either to ford or ride five miles out of my course to reach a bridge. My horse was a powerful animal, but untried as a swimmer. I was not easily intimidated; and though there had been recent heavy rains, I determined to risk the ford. I found the water higher than I anticipated, but dared not halt to consider, lest my nerve should fail and I be forced to return and seek the bridge. I urged my horse into the stream and, to my surprise and his dismay, found the water beyond his depth. Instead of adjusting himself for a swim, he began to plunge, frenzied with fright. Seeing that horse and rider were likely to perish in the swollen stream, I slipped from the saddle and succeeded in floundering back to the bank. The frightened animal, now released of his burden, took courage and, following my example, reached the shore in safety. Nearly exhausted, I sat down, panting for breath, and thanked God for deliverance. I returned home a wiser and wetter man, and after a readjustment I took the longer and safer route across the bridge.

Clinton Circuit was a four weeks' work, of one hundred and fifty miles, with twenty-seven appointments, which required a sermon for almost every day in the month.

CHAPTER IV.

Army Life.

> The bursting shell, the gateway wrenched asunder,
>   The rattling musketry, the clashing blade,
> And ever and anon in tones of thunder
>   The diapason of the cannonade.   —*Longfellow.*

I HAD made perhaps half a round on my circuit when I was suddenly and strangely impressed that duty called me to the Confederate army. Being satisfied that God was leading me, I neither sought nor needed any other guide. I quietly left the work and traveled alone on horseback to Tupelo, Miss., where I found General Forrest's mounted infantry encamped. The Eighth Kentucky Regiment, commanded by Col. A. R. Shacklett, was without a chaplain. The Colonel seemed glad to meet me and said: "Parson, I hope you will have a good influence over our boys. They need you. Consider yourself in charge of this regiment."

This was my initiation into army life. And without formality, commission, or salary I entered service and went into camp. I knew the mild outdoor life would bring a change and would soon improve my health or end an existence which had been one of almost constant suffering for years. The change, though doubtful for a time, soon proved beneficial, and I gained strength for service.

I was illy prepared to interest or edify the men, many of whom were educated and judges of preaching; but when opportunity offered I held services, and they always gave me a respectful and attentive hearing. On one occasion while encamped I held a series of services. We worshiped in nature's temple, including all out-of-doors; while the moon gave us light, the earth furnished seats, and the trunk of a fallen tree served as a mourners' bench. Here in the moonlit forest I witnessed a wonderful work of grace in the deep conviction and sound conversion of a number of young men of the regiment, some of whom lived but a few brief days; but they were ready and went over and up to join the "choir invisible."

I had the privilege of ministering to many who were sick or wounded and saw many converted in the wayside hospitals during the year.

My initiation into the horrors of war was a call to carry a death sentence to three young men who were condemned to be shot to death with musketry at four o'clock one afternoon. I received the order at nine in the morning. One of the three was reprieved at the grave. The other two, handcuffed together, were executed. One of them constantly cried and prayed for mercy; the other made no demonstration. He was perfectly calm and said to me: "I regret to die in this way and am sorry that my parents will know that I have been executed. But I am not afraid to die. I am under twenty-one years of age. I was living at home with my parents and was at church on the Sabbath when a squad of soldiers surrounded the church and took me, with other boys, by force and put us into the army. I lived in a State which had not seceded from the Union, and therefore I felt that

I had a right to go back to my home. I made the effort and was captured, and now I am to die. But I was converted when I was fourteen years of age, have tried to live a Christian life, and now have peace with God." He then gave me directions to write to his parents of his death and requested that his funeral sermon be at his home church. Then giving me special messages to members of his family, he bade me good-by, and as the tears rolled down his quiet face he simply said: "I will soon be happier than those whom I leave." In a few moments the fatal volley sent the two spirits into the other life.

The impression has remained with me. I can see how a person advanced in years and weary with constant suffering might grow tired of life and be willing to meet death calmly, simply as a release from pain and unrest. But when I saw this youth in the prime of life, buoyant with health, with the prospect of a long life before him, calmly face death, it assured me that there is a sustaining power in simple faith in Christ to be found nowhere else.

I witnessed many sad and pathetic scenes—men dying away from home and loved ones—but some of the most triumphant deaths I ever witnessed were under those conditions. I was much with the wounded and the dying, and amid it all I enjoyed daily communion with God and now have the pleasant assurance that it was one of the most useful periods of my life.

I shall here relate a strange incident. I simply give it for what it is worth and leave to others the explanation.

Autobiography of Bishop Henry Clay Morrison.

Late in 1864 there came to the brigade a friend of mine from Western Kentucky. He left a family at home and had been with the army only a few days when he received the impression that he would be killed. He sought an interview with me and told me, as a confidential friend, of his presentiment. I tried to treat the matter lightly and laugh him out of the notion. I said to him: "You have not yet smelled gunpowder. Wait until you have gone through one or two battles, and you will get free from this impression." My words of ridicule had no effect. He still insisted that he would be killed very soon. He said: "I have about three hundred dollars in United States money which I wish you to send back to my family after my death. I shall conceal it in the lining of my boot leg, where you can find it. Will you promise me to do this?" I told him that if I were living at the time I would comply with his request. I then added: "If I were in your place and felt as you do, I would not go into battle under such an impression. I would go to my commander and tell him my feeling and ask to be relieved until I was in a better state of mind." "No," he said, "the matter is fixed. And while I feel a strange solemnity, I am not distressed. All I wish is the promise from you."

That was ten o'clock at night. The army moved in the early morning and was in battle by noon. My friend's regiment was held for a time in reserve and when ordered to the front marched by the field hospital, where I was engaged with the wounded and dying. He waved to me as he passed, went to the front, and was dead on the field in less than an hour.

This was less than twenty hours after he had said to me: "I shall be killed very soon."

Facts like the above occur, I know, but do not understand. One thing is certain: there is little space between us and the unknown world, and we sometimes receive impressions from that mystic land.

CHAPTER V.

PEACE AND ITS FRUITAGE.

O, there were hours when thrilling joy repaid
  A long, long course of darkness, doubts, and fears—
The heartsick faintness of the hope delayed,
  The waste, the woe, the bloodshed, and the tears
  That tracked with terror the bloody rolling years!
                                                —*Scott.*

IN the spring of 1865, after peace was declared, I was employed as assistant preacher to Rev. H. C. Settle on the Logan Circuit, in the Louisville Conference, and was admitted on trial into that Conference the following September.

The Conference was held at Russellville, Bishop Kavanaugh presiding. From that Conference I was appointed to Millerstown Circuit, which embraced portions of Hart, Grayson, and Hardin Counties. Much of the territory was very poor, and the people were generally poor, but were kind-hearted and loved their preacher.

It was a year of much physical suffering. While my experience in the army had been a benefit, I was far from being in robust health. However, I met my appointments, held protracted meetings, and saw numbers converted. I succeeded a man who was greatly beloved by the people, and on my first visit to the home of a good brother his wife inquired as to where they had sent Brother H——, my predecessor. I kindly told her where he had been sent. She replied: "I wish they had sent him back to us." To which I responded: "I wish so too, madam." But it was only a short time until the good, motherly soul was as much attached to me as she had been to her previous pastor.

It is an easy matter for a Methodist preacher to gain the confidence of his people if he has the spirit of the Master.

I was holding a meeting in a rude schoolhouse in what was known as the "Sand Hills." It was a day of fasting and prayer, and I had eaten nothing that day and preached twice. At the night service, after preaching, I spent an hour with penitents at the altar. At ten o'clock, when the service closed, a good old woman, who had come three miles to service, invited me to go home with her to see her afflicted husband. A slow, chilly rain was falling, and, tired as I was, nothing remained for me but to go. I found my way in the darkness to my horse and was about to mount, when I heard a scream. I turned and saw by the light of a torch that the horse on which the old lady was mounted had reared and fallen backward, crushing the rider into unconsciousness. I ordered her carried back into the schoolhouse, where I spread my shawl on the floor in front of the smoldering fire, took from my pocket a flask of brandy and wild cherry, which my physician ordered me to carry with me and use three times daily, and dosed the old lady until she was so limber that she could not have ridden horseback even if she had not been hurt.

A messenger was sent for a physician, eight miles away, and necessity required that he use my saddle for the trip. Another messenger went to the home of the old lady for a conveyance; and at one o'clock in the morning the conveyance arrived, but no doctor. The woman was placed on a bed in the vehicle, surrounded by others to care for her. One country girl, who had come on foot, was unprovided for. I mounted my horse without a saddle, took the girl up behind me, and started in the darkness on a slow, tedious trip of three miles. The roadway was a succession of steep hills and deep hollows. Delicate in health and weak from fasting since the previous day, I was well-nigh exhausted; and having no saddle, going slowly down a long, steep hill, with my own weight and that of my feminine partner pressing against me, and my hands grappling the heavy mane of my horse to prevent us both from taking a "header," it was a picture worthy of a comic artist. It was well that darkness shut out the scene. When I could no longer prop with safety, I would turn the head of my horse uphill until we could slide backward and adjust ourselves for another siege.

At three o'clock in the morning we reached the good old woman's humble home. The young preacher felt more dead than alive. The experience of that night lingers in my memory as one of the trying ordeals of my early ministry.

It was on this my first charge that I witnessed some things not common at this day, but frequent in the religious demonstration of the earlier days. I was conducting a series of meetings in a schoolhouse when it pleased God to give me a wonderful baptism of the Holy Spirit by which I was lifted up so closely in touch with the supernatural that I had but little thought of material things. I was floating in what seemed to me a fathomless sea of peace and joy. This quiet, ecstatic state continued without abatement for perhaps four weeks. It was during this time that I saw the unusual religious demonstrations. In some instances penitents at the altar became unconscious and lay as if dead for an hour, and even for hours, but when consciousness returned they invariably rejoiced and praised God.

On one occasion I was preaching at a morning service to a crowded house, with numbers standing before the door and at the windows, when suddenly a stalwart young man standing in full view fell to the earth as if pierced with a rifle ball. He lay for an hour or more speechless and almost pulseless. But when he came to himself he sprang to his feet and, with a peculiar brightness on his face, shouted the praises of God. I witnessed another similar case at that meeting. And here I wish to record that under my preaching, while I was under the baptism of the Spirit, there was an almost irresistible power. It was never so at any other time. And if we as preachers would keep so close to God as to be ever under this influence, would not his word truly "run and be glorified" and a veritable Pentecost be repeated in these later days?

My principal home for that year was with a Pennsylvania family of the name of Jenkins, at Uptonville, Ky. They were plain but excellent and godly people, who did me many kindnesses and became my lifetime friends.

While on this circuit my health at times seemed hopelessly gone. My friends thought I was the victim of consumption. But with a naturally cheerful spirit and an indomitable will, I clung tenaciously to life. The pain in the chest was steady and unabating and the night sweats profuse; but, using blisters and counter-irritants, I kept going and refused to surrender.

One morning, when the kind family thought I was past going, without my knowledge they called in a physician, who found my circulation forty-five per minute and remarked: "You are the feeblest man I have ever seen walking." Evidently the family believed I was going to die, and that hundreds of miles from my father's home. A son-in-law in the home, a generous Baptist brother, came into my room and after some circumlocution said: "Brother Morrison, if you would like to go home and rest until you get stronger and have not the money, I will let you have all you need." I smiled and said: "You are very kind; but I am not going to die here on your hands." I shall never forget the blush of mingled kindness and confusion when he saw that I had read his mind. He has long since gone to the other life, but I have ever held him in affectionate remembrance.

About this time there came into the community two strange men claiming to heal all manner of diseases. Many good people were led to have confidence in their claims, and numerous instances were cited of their power to heal the sick. A friend insisted that I "give him a trial." I laughed at the idea. But he urged me earnestly and insisted that it would not hurt me, and he would not be satisfied until I gave them a trial. Accordingly I called on them and met two rough and rustic specimens of the *genus homo*.

One of them remarked that I did not look as if I could stand severe treatment. We repaired to a schoolhouse in a grove near by. The day was warm, and they bade me lay off my coat and be seated on a rude bench near a window. They then began to walk to and fro, passing me and gesticulating in a peculiar manner and at the same time expressing fear that I was too weak to bear much of the healing influence or power.

After proceeding for a time they asked me if I felt any effect. I replied: "I feel the effect of the breeze from the window." This seemed to provoke them, and they said: "We can cure you if you will take the risk." I said: "Gentlemen, if you have any power, throw it upon me, and all you have at that." They began to rush to and fro and gesticulate as frantically as Baal's prophets under the sarcastic jeers of Elijah. After keeping this up until they were well-nigh exhausted, they asked if I was satisfied. I replied: "I am satisfied that you have no power to affect me in any way whatever." They said: "We are satisfied if you will pay us one dollar." This I did and left them.

I give this as a specimen of the fakes with which society has ever been cursed by creatures too lazy to work and duping the people by pretending to have power with God. All such fakery, whether in the name of faith-healing or Christian Science, so called, or else, is but the stealing of "the livery of the court of heaven to serve the devil in," although some of the cult may be honest dupes of their own delusion.

After a revival in one of the several schoolhouses, I became enthused with the idea of a church at that place. There was little money to be had, but there were splendid trees in the forest and stalwart men to fell and hew them. So I proceeded to canvass the community to find out how much work I could secure.

Coming at noontime to a home where the family were at dinner, I was kindly invited to dine with them; but as I was in haste and too full of my enterprise to lose time in dining, I declined. But noticing on the table a fine dish of sweet potatoes, I concluded to take one and eat it as I rode. On the way I proceeded to attack the potato, which I found to be cold. Eating rather rapidly, and failing to remember that the clammy and adhesive nature of a cold potato added to my enervated condition, I suddenly found that my throat was clogged and I was on the point of choking to death. I was on the brow of a little hill, and, looking down before me, I saw some hogs in a mud wallow at the foot of the hill. Spurring my horse, I went down the hill at desperate speed. The frightened swine fled from the puddle, and I fell from my horse with my face in the foul water and managed to swallow enough of it to remove the obstruction and save my life. But for this mudhole I would have ended my ministerial life in a few moments. I have ever been grateful for this providential deliverance, although the means were not the most æsthetic.

I was a child of nature and full of enthusiasm. I had a way of acting my sermons in the pulpit, and I fear there was far more action than thought. This was especially true when speaking of anything partaking of the tragic. The effect at times was remarkable. The visitors would crowd the church or school-

Autobiography of Bishop Henry Clay Morrison.

house and stand in numbers at the windows on the outside. Giving a graphic description of hell on one occasion and quoting Pollock very freely, a godless young man in the audience sprang to his feet and would have fled from the place had not a friend held him and compelled him to be seated. He declared to his friend that "no preacher ought to be allowed to uncap hell after that manner in public."

Wild and extravagant stories of the wonderful young circuit rider were soon afloat, and at the following Conference session I was interviewed by the distinguished Dr. John H. Linn and asked if I would consent to be sent to the city of Louisville. At first I thought it a joke of this great and good man's, but he was in dead earnest and said: "We have heard all about you, and you will go to Louisville if you will consent."

I told him I had only about half a dozen sermons, that they were mere things, small and inconsiderable, and that I would by no means consent to be sent to the city. I said: "Doctor, I know myself better than you know me. Please have me sent to some light work, where I will not be exposed to inclement weather and where I can gain strength enough to live and learn how to preach." He looked at me, with my bloodless face and cadaverous features, and said kindly: "Perhaps you are right."

I was sent to Bardstown, a small station in Nelson County. It was six years before I was sent to Louisville, and that was too soon, I fear, for the interest of the Church.

I relate this incident for the benefit of such young

preachers as may be tempted to seek premature promotion. Many a young man has been well-nigh ruined by too much puffing and pushing while in his swaddling clothes. I soon learned that "bodily exercise profiteth little," and I quit dramatizing the gospel.

This first year on the Millerstown Circuit was one of constant labor and almost incessant suffering, but I had the joy of seeing numbers converted at each of the appointments on the charge. When I received my appointment to this my first charge, I did not once think of what I was to receive. They paid me $160 for the year, and I felt then and have ever felt that they paid liberally, considering the quality of the preaching they received. When I was paid my first money I felt embarrassed, as if I had not the right to accept it. Such, I believe, was the common experience of young men entering the ministry at that period.

But I fear there has been a change at this point, inasmuch as I now hear the young preacher ask: "What does it pay?" I regard this as no good indication of a preacher's desire to do good. The young preacher should go to his work not thinking of what the people can do for him, but of what he can do for them and for the Master.

There is one question that should settle all other questions with the itinerant preacher. It is this: "Has God called me to the work? Am I really moved by the Holy Ghost to take upon me the work of this ministry?" Being sure of this, all other questions are settled. God will not call me to work a failure. Let me do what God directs, and he will provide for my temporal necessities. If I meet hardship and suffering, that does not prove that I am not going God's way. Daniel was going God's way when he landed in the den, and the Hebrew children were not out of the path of duty when they found a fiery furnace in their way. Paul, when he went to prison and to death, and the Son of God, when he went to the cross, together with the "hundred and forty and four thousand" who were seen in white robes before the throne, "all came up through great tribulation" as they traveled along the path of duty. The path of duty is often the path of danger.

Before leaving the field of my first year's labor, I shall record a little incident ever memorable in the village of Millerstown, from which the circuit took its name. It was a notable affair of honor which occurred there in the earlier days of the town. One William Bowman, a local preacher, familiarly known as "Bill" Bowman, gave offense to a young man of high mettle by reproving him publicly for misconduct in church. The offense was followed immediately by a challenge for a duel. Bowman promptly accepted the challenge, and, being the challenged party, he claimed the right under the code to choose the weapons and the distance for the contest. The weapons chosen were one peck of Irish potatoes, each to be no less in size than a man's fist, and the distance fifteen paces.

The young man protested, but Bowman forced him to the terms. The hour was appointed, and the citizens were out in numbers to witness the duel. The young man, deeply mortified, was on hand.

Bowman was a backwoodsman and could throw a stone with the force and accuracy of a catapult, and the result was that each missile he threw struck his antagonist with such force as to burst it and raise knots various and sundry where knots counted most. When the poor fellow had endured five or six such strokes, he cried out with pain and gave up the fight. His punishment was sufficient to put him to bed and call for the services of a physician.

The citizens of the town to this day delight to tell of "Bill Bowman's duel," and we would here recommend the same weapons and distance in every "affair of honor."

CHAPTER VI.

Marriage and Home Life.

To love, to bliss their blended souls were given;
And each, too happy, asked no brighter heaven.
—*Dwight.*

Bardstown, Ky., was my second charge. It was an old site of learning, and the people were cultured and refined. Our Church there was not strong, but its membership was of the very best element. I felt as if I should sit at the feet of my flock rather than be their spiritual leader and teacher. Only God knew with what fear and trembling I undertook this work. But the good people, ever considerate of my inability and lack of experience, with numerous other lacks, gave me encouragement and helped me after a sort to fill the place of preacher in charge.

One incident in my experience there has influenced my entire ministerial life. I was born with an independence of spirit which has stood me well in many trying ordeals and remains with me to this day. And I have little hope for the young man in any avocation in life who is without it.

It was a dreary December afternoon, made worse by an east wind. I had been out on a round of pastoral duty and was wearily plodding my way back to my boarding house when Satan set me to soliloquizing. I said to myself: "Here I am without a dollar, hundreds of miles from home, half sick, and almost staggering from physical weakness. I have on the only pair of trousers I possess, and they are threadbare, so that I have to be careful lest they yield in places even to raggedness. I was making money as a teacher before I gave up my avocation to serve this people, who care nothing for me." In the midst of this wicked soliloquy I became so wrought up that I gritted my teeth and almost murmured at the providence that had sent me to such a hard service.

In this rebellious and unhappy state of mind I reached my room and found a letter containing for me a five-dollar bank note from a kind-hearted old lady. Imagine my feelings. I was stunned, rebuked, humbled, and subdued. I closed my room door and, falling upon my knees before God, prayed and wept until I felt that he had forgiven my sad lack of faith and my wicked spirit of rebellion. From that hour until this, more than forty years, I have been able to leave all with him, and he has kept me from even a momentary impulse of dissatisfaction with my lot.

Stoner's Chapel, perhaps nine miles from Bardstown, was attached to the station and was, therefore, a part of the Bardstown work. One Sabbath in each month was given to the chapel. It was here that the young preacher met his fate and fortune. Mr. J. P. Stoner, who built the chapel and lived near it, had an only daughter, a young widow with two small children. Like Mohammed and Washington, I fell a victim to the widow's charms, and we were married in the year 1868. Forty years have rolled their course along time's causeway since we began life's journey together, and to my companion I owe much for any measure of success attending my ministry.

God has given us seven children. Five of them have passed to the other life, while two of them remain with us—Horace T. Morrison, a business man, and Henry K. Morrison, a young physician. Both reside at Leesburg, Fla., and are living in the faith of the gospel. The five who are waiting for us died with heaven in view and will greet us when we go. The two stepchildren, Eugene B. Ray and Mrs. Lillie McClaskey, we reared as our own, and their devotion and affection have ever been as if they were our own. They have reared families in their own comfortable Kentucky homes and are living in the service of God and in the hope of immortality.

The year at Bardstown was not eventful. A number, however, were converted and added to the Church.

At the following Annual Conference I was stationed at Elizabethtown, Ky., and was the first preacher ever placed in that station. Here a most remarkable revival occurred within a few weeks after the Conference session. It was one of those visitations of divine power which always constitutes an epoch in the history of a Church, a time to which the members afterwards refer and from which they date many things in the years that follow.

It was winter, and the weather was fearfully inclement; "but the multitudes flocked to the place." Many came for miles through snow, rain, and darkness. The church was crowded day and night beyond its capacity. The Divine Presence hung over the town, like the cloud over Israel's camp, for twenty-two days. People were converted in their homes and at their places of business, and the work continued until ninety-eight souls found peace with God.

The wealthiest man in the charge, and a genuinely spiritual man, was at the head of a wholesale whisky house. He was true to his Church, punctual at family prayers, and unquestioned in his Christian integrity. But he was under the delusion that there was no wrong in dealing in whisky. He was my personal friend and paid a large part of my salary; but I loved him too dearly to leave him alone in his dangerous delusion. After frequent talks and much prayer with him without avail, I said to him kindly: "If I can neither argue nor pray you out of the whisky business, I can, by the help of God, preach you out of it." He laughed and said he would come to hear me. And he came. And God was there also. There was a strange and deathlike silence under the message. It was an awful hour with the multitudes that crowded the church. When the services closed, the people silently dispersed, as if under the spell of some mystic power.

Although I was boarding in the home of this brother, I did not meet him the next morning either at morning prayers or the morning meal; nor did he let me meet him at noon. But I determined to know his state of mind, and in the afternoon I went directly to his place of business. As I entered the building he came forward to meet me and, throwing his arms about me, sobbingly said: "I am not angry with you. I wish to say that I never saw what I was doing until last night. I am winding up my business to-day, and I will never handle another gallon of whisky as long as I live." And he never did.

Autobiography of Bishop Henry Clay Morrison.

His health afterwards failed, and he took a trip for a change of climate with the hope of improvement. In the meantime I had been sent to another field of labor. He left a request that in case of his death I should officiate at his funeral. He died while away, and I responded to the call. We buried him in the home cemetery, with two thousand people gathered at his grave. We buried him with clean hands and a pure heart, and his name is a precious memory.

I give this incident to encourage young preachers to make no compromise with the rum traffic. When the devotees of this evil would intimate that you are out of your sphere and meddling with politics, I wish to advise you, and leave my advice on record when I am gone, that if fighting the rum traffic is going into politics, then go and stay in politics until the liquor curse is driven from the American republic. The whisky question is a moral question, and you have a right to follow every moral question, whether it gets into politics or into the sea.

I may add just here that I came near losing my life in the same town while on my way to church on a very dark night. Coming in contact with a burly Irishman who was frenzied with strong drink and striking madly about him with a knife, he attacked me. The darkness prevented me from seeing the knife. He grasped me and continued his strokes with the knife. Fortunately, I had in my hand a large walking cane, which I used vigorously until I extricated myself from his grasp and prostrated him. When the fray was over, I found that my right arm had a deep and dangerous knife wound, and my cloth-

Autobiography of Bishop Henry Clay Morrison.

ing was cut to ruins. Now, this poor wretch had no ill will toward me, but was simply a maniac from strong drink and incapable of knowing the nature of his own conduct.

No man is a true friend to his own family, community, or country who will not vote and work against the manufacture, sale, and use of intoxicating liquor.

The two years at Elizabethtown were memorable for the manifestations of the saving power of the gospel. The membership of the Church was doubled, and the fruits of those years remain after the passing of four decades.

My next appointment was to the Middletown charge, composed of three churches—namely, Middletown, O'Bannon, and Rudy's Chapel. All were within a few miles of Louisville. Here I served for three years, and here, too, I found lighter work and lighter piety. The people were kind and generous, but not deeply spiritual. Hence the pastor had but little aid in any of the public services. I loved those people, and the memory of their friendship lingers with me. Their generous donations of the necessaries of life nearly supported the then small family, leaving the salary of $1,000 to be expended otherwise. At this place I had the lightest work and more spending money than at any time in my itinerant life, although in after years I received as much as $4,000.

I have found this to be true: If the Methodist Church pays a pastor $500, he is expected to live on that amount; if he is paid $5,000, he is expected to spend it in some form of Church enterprise. And so the itinerant and his wife must learn the all-important lesson of "cutting the garment to fit the cloth." Should he leave even small debts unpaid, his influence is soon damaged, if not destroyed. If he makes special effort to accumulate money, he is likely to be dubbed a "money preacher," and his influence for good is at an end.

CHAPTER VII.

CITY LIFE.

Here laden carts with thundering wagons meet;
Wheels clash with wheels and bar the narrow street.
—*Gay*.

AFTER three pleasant years at Middletown, I was unexpectedly sent to Shelby Street charge, in the city of Louisville, in the autumn of 1872. Here I found an unusually religious people with very little of that commendable Church pride which is so essential to the success of a Church. The building was dilapidated and a discredit to the membership, who believed themselves too poor to repair it. But there were in the Church godly women with hearts full of love for Christ and hands ready to work for his cause. Largely through their faith and work the church was repaired at a cost of $3,000 and the pastor's salary increased from $1,000 to $1,800. Much of the money raised to repair the church was due to the women of the Church, who ran a lunch house for several days and realized $800 as the result of their work.

The matter of lunches and suppers for Church purposes has been much discussed, and, like many other questions, it has more than one side. There is a medium ground on this and kindred matters which is generally the safer ground, and it is a good idea to "keep in the middle of the road."

We should have nothing to do with anything that has the semblance of sin. Let lotteries, raffles, and grab bags alone. Encourage nothing that has the "appearance of evil." There are those with hearts to help the Church. Godly women who have no money will solicit contributions of material and then prepare and serve food at a fair price to business men who patronize them and get the worth of the money they spend in a substantial meal. Such work is legitimate and helpful. In this way women contribute to the Church, which they could not otherwise do, and at the same time they encourage the social feature and have the joy of ministering to the Master while they minister to others.

During my pastorate at Shelby Street Church one of life's longed-for opportunities came. Up to this time I had never taken a lesson in any of the dead languages. The Rev. N. H. Lee, D.D., was at that time the presiding elder of the Louisville District. He was a man of marked ability, an experienced teacher of languages, and enjoyed his work as a teacher. I was fortunate in having him as an inmate of my home for four years. After procuring two sets of Latin and Greek books, I set up a sort of university of my own. At the end of the day I would sit over those books until the midnight hour and even later. Carrying a heavy charge, making sermons, doing the pastoral work, studying the languages at night, in feeble health, and a constant sufferer, I sometimes would stagger, as I walked, from sheer lack of strength. But I knew that it was the one opportunity to get the longed-for knowledge so much needed by every preacher of the gospel. Therefore I pressed on until I secured a fair knowledge of Latin and Greek, and even of Hebrew to a limited extent, but sufficient to be helpful in my ministry.

I rejoice that now facilities are far better for young men without means to secure an education, and I advise every young preacher to get a knowledge of the languages if he can. It will give him confidence and added force to be able to examine the root of the texts and know that he has the very thoughts that were in the mind of the Spirit when he indited the words.

It was during my pastorate at Shelby Street that an experience came to me which I record with profound gratitude to God.

While serving as junior preacher supply for a short time on the Logan Circuit, previous to my admission on trial in the Conference, I contracted the habit of smoking cigars. Seven years' indulgence had developed an appetite for tobacco that rendered me a slave to the habit. Realizing the power of the appetite, I resolved, like Samson, to rise up and break the withes that bound me and be free; but, like him, I found myself shorn of my strength.

In my extremity I went to God in prayer, believing that he would help me to gradually get free from my bondage. I promised on my knees to give up the habit, broke the promise, repeated it from time to time, only to break my resolution. I fought hard and long, but invariably fell. I would throw away my cigars and desperately resolve to go through at least one night without a smoke, and at midnight I would search the lumber room of the parsonage for tobacco leaves which had been placed among the packed clothing as a protection from the moths. These I would roll into cigars and would smoke them. It seemed during my abstinence as if I would go mad if I did not get tobacco. Knowing, as I do, what it is to be in bondage to this habit, I know how to sympathize with my fellow men who are in the merciless grasp of this appetite.

After fighting and failing and falling until I was unwilling and ashamed to go back to God with my worthless vows, I finally surrendered to what I believed to be my unalterable fate. I gave up the struggle and resigned myself to my doom—a tobacco slave.

I had then a temporary rest—such, I presume, as comes to the impenitent after long suffering under conviction, when the conscience becomes seared and the soul past feeling. But in the good providence of God I was not to remain in this state.

Not long after my "surrender" a friend sent me a small tract entitled "The Wonders of Grace in the Instantaneous Deliverance from the Whisky, Opium, and Tobacco Habits." This was to me an entirely new thought. The "instantaneous" deliverance! I had prayed and hoped for gradual relief, but the idea of being delivered instantly had never entered my mind.

The first thought was: "This is fanaticism." However, I sat down to reason the matter out with myself. I had at that moment a half-consumed cigar in my fingers, and no less than ten or fifteen cigars per day would satisfy my craving. I asked myself: Do I believe what I preach? I do. Do I not preach to the sinner that God will take away the sins of a whole lifetime in an instant if he will ask and believe. I do, and I know by experience that this is true. Then if God can and will take away the sins of a lifetime in an instant, can he not in an instant and will he not take away an appetite which I have been only seven years in forming? Again: Do I not preach that "whatsoever ye ask, that is consistent with his will, and believe that ye receive it, ye shall have it"? I do believe and preach all this. Then is it not consistent with the divine will that I should be free from this merciless appetite that is injuring me? Yes, I believe God is willing. Then came the hard question, *Am I willing?* If God can and will take away this appetite, am I willing that he should do it? I had suffered so much that my whole being, soul and body, answered, "Yes, yes." Instantly I found it according to my faith. The chain broke, and deliverance came. The cigar passed out of my fingers and the craving out of my life. I was consciously free. There were no discomforts from the sudden ending of the indulgence, no stupor, no craving, no nervous unrest, no disquiet whatever. I was as a little child who had never known the use of a narcotic.

More than forty years have passed since then, and there has never been from that time the faintest desire for tobacco in any form.

I write the above as a debtor to grace, that it may be helpful to some poor soul who is in bondage and who longs for freedom.

If we would but take God at his word, believe him as we believe a friend, cease to philosophize and trust him as a little child would trust the word of its father, then would our religion be a daily joy and life a real "walk with God."

Autobiography of Bishop Henry Clay Morrison.

The time has come when the use of tobacco discounts a minister. The fact no longer can be ridiculed or laughed to silence. When a good mother has taught her children that a preacher is the best of men and that when he comes he will talk about Jesus and how to be good and at the same time teaches them that the use of tobacco is wrong, unclean, and hurtful, then when the preacher comes to the home and the sharp eyes of childhood see the minister addicted to the use of a thing that they have always been taught is wrong, what must the children think? And how can such conduct be satisfactorily explained?

If you as a young preacher are already enslaved, go at once to God in prayer and simple trust and be free. "If the Son shall make you free, you shall be free indeed."

The spiritual life of the Church at Shelby Street charge was such that conversions were frequent at the regular services, and the old-time class meetings were regularly attended. It was during my pastorate here that I was called to Shelbyville, Ky., to assist the pastor, Rev. John R. Deering, in a meeting. Shelbyville is an old site of learning, and the people are refined and cultured.

The meeting opened on Sabbath morning with the writer in the pulpit. There was only fair liberty. The sermon was moderate and the visible impression limited. The sermon at night was with less liberty. Monday night there was still less liberty, and by Tuesday there was no liberty at all. The power to preach seemed to be entirely gone. It was a strange experience and one which had never come to me before. I was not conscious of any sin that would sever me from the source of power. I was bewildered, but not humiliated. I felt willing to be nothing if only God's cause could be honored.

Under the most profound sense of helplessness I stood before that intelligent audience and said: "I cannot preach. I cannot tell why. I will not take a text nor make another trial. I will stand up in my Master's name and talk to the people." This I did from night to night, and before the week passed God had shaken that town as never before by the power of his Spirit. Nearly twenty souls were powerfully converted, and the whole town was brought under the influence of revival power. Never have I witnessed more clearly that it is "not my might, nor by power, but my Spirit, saith the Lord."

Let us but give ourselves as preachers fully to Christ; and whether we be exalted or abased, he will use us to the saving of men.

At the close of a successful quadrennium at Shelby Street I was sent to Broadway, at that time considered the leading Church in Louisville Methodism. I entered upon the work with a full consciousness of my inability, but with faith in God and a firm belief that my weakness could be made the background for showing forth his power. This Church had an elegant membership of refined people. Some of them were really spiritually-minded, but there was much of the conventional in the Church service. The choir was made up largely of professionals, who cared little for the worship except to perform their part. There was enough of the formal and conventional to produce chilliness in the public service, which is unfriendly to religious joy and destructive of that simplicity which characterized Methodism in the early days of its power.

While I met with courtesy and kindness, yet the new pastor suffered as if he were in the frigid zone of ecclesiasticism. To preach with liberty seemed almost impossible, and it was only after months of prayer and soul agony that God broke the fetters, and I came into freedom. But the fetters were broken and fell from preacher and people. Power came down, the Church was baptized, and nearly one hundred souls were converted to God.

There is nothing more pleasing to the devil than to have a Church burdened with a sense of its own respectability and frozen to zero by a soulless formalism.

There is a certain simplicity essential to our success as Methodists, and every departure from that simplicity is a loss of power. We may add to our Ritual and enlarge our Order of Service, but this only detracts from that humility which "has its own way with God." These additions may be increased until they are burdensome and we have "more harness than horse." "Where the Spirit of the Lord is, there is liberty." And his Spirit only can give power in preaching and liberty in worship.

While at Broadway I witnessed a conversion that I consider somewhat remarkable. The Bourbon Stockyards was a place where the blue-grass stock was bought and sold, a place where much money was handled and where the traders generally seemed as if "God were not in all their thoughts." Among those godless money changers was one George C——. He was a man who had no thought or care for anything beyond the material. The making of money was the one motive in his life. He was perhaps thirty-five years of age, large, handsome, and a splendid specimen of manhood. I knew him but slightly, but on one occasion he accosted me on the street and said: "I wish to talk with you about religion." My first thought was that he was jesting, but in a moment I saw that he was in earnest. "When can I see you?" he asked. "To-morrow at my home," I replied. He was there promptly and under deep conviction. We prayed together as he wept. Then he asked when he could join the Church. I told him he could join on the following Sabbath. Said he: "Can I join at the midweek prayer meeting, without waiting until Sunday?" I told him he could, and on the following Wednesday night he sat with his wife in the rear of the audience, and when the invitation was given they both came forward and were received into the Church.

On reaching home that night he read the Bible and offered prayer for his family, which consisted of himself, wife, and two children. This practice he kept up daily.

The news was soon circulated at the stockyards that George C—— had professed religion and joined the Church. His godless associates immediately began to jeer him and make sport of his pretension. He said: "Gentlemen, that is all right. Make as much sport of me as you wish; I deserve it all. But from this time forward I intend to serve the Lord." His companions saw his sincerity and at once changed their conduct and showed him the most marked respect.

Six weeks from the time he joined the Church we buried him. The mention of his name at the stockyards after this was always in a minor key, and the influence of his brief Christian life abides as a helpful inspiration at that place. Later I found the secret of his remarkable conversion. It was a godly mother, whose prayers had followed him from infancy. Let no mother lose heart and give up her wayward boy so long as she has access to the mercy seat.

My pastorate at Broadway was an epoch in my life. Broadway at that time was regarded as the leading Church of our denomination in the State. My appointment to it was like putting a man in a rudderless ship on a shoreless sea and demanding that he find his way to land. I had exhausted my little stock of sermons at Shelby Street charge and would now have to preach to some of the same people; hence I was compelled to have two new sermons every Sunday.

The great Dr. Hall, when asked how many sermons a preacher could make in a week, made this reply: "If he is an extraordinary man, he can make one; if he is a mediocre, he can make two; but if he is an ass, he can make a dozen."

I got my reckoning as a mediocre and proceeded to produce two sermons a week for four years at this charge and also during a like term at my next charge. Many of these sermons were quite small, but I passed them off under the name of sermons. They were never used the second time, and now after forty years I am sending them through the Church press under the name of "Gospel Talks," and God is blessing them to the help of many of the common people and the shut-ins and such as cannot attend the preaching of the Word.

At the close of the term at Broadway I was appointed to Chestnut Street, in the same city, one of our standard Churches, which had been served by some of our best and most representative men. Here I found a cultivated and godly people, with whom I spent four years of service, saw many converted to God, and secured a valuable parsonage for my successor.

I was then sent, in 1884, to Russellville, Ky., the site of the Logan Female College, having served twelve years in the three Louisville Churches. At Russellville I found an excellent but not a wealthy people. The Church was limited in its financial strength and was able to pay the pastor less than half the amount he had been receiving for years.

Here I wish to say, for the benefit of any pastor who may be sent to a reduced salary, that the salary is not all. The love of the people, their friendship, and their little gifts from time to time—all these things are helpful. I never loved a people more nor had a happier pastorate than this, which could pay less than half my previous salary.

It was here that an expression of devotion to his pastor was made by a man with a large family who said: "I would rather do without meat on my table than for our pastor to leave us." This statement, not made in my hearing, was all the more appreciated and touched me more deeply than anything ever said of me in my ministry. Such indications of love cause us to forget abbreviated salaries and other hardships of the itinerant life.

After two years and three months with this lovely people, I was unexpectedly transferred to the North Georgia Conference and stationed at First Church, Atlanta. Here I found a membership of about one thousand first-class people. God honored his word, though spoken in weakness, from the beginning to the close of this pastorate. At the first service two prominent citizens, advanced in life, gave themselves to God. This was the beginning of a revival which continued for three years and a half. The church, which would seat comfortably one thousand people, was crowded and persons were turned away at almost every service. I have seen five hundred souls in the weekly prayer meeting. Conversions were common at the regular Sunday services. Strangers were impressed with a sense of the Divine Presence, which seemed to abide. It was neither attractive music nor pulpit oratory that drew the crowds, but God was there. Multitudes flocked to the place, because, as at Pentecost, the Holy Ghost fell on the people. I have passed a ministry of more than fifty years and have witnessed many manifestations of divine power, but First Church, Atlanta, was the mightiest spiritual force I have ever known.

It was at this time that the immortal Henry Grady was reclaimed. He had been a Church member from early life, but had grown spiritually cold and indifferent. In response to a public invitation given at the Sunday morning service he came to the chancel and, reaching his hand to the pastor, addressed the audience while still holding the pastor's hand, made a confession of his lost time, and pledged his fidelity to Christ for the time to come. He remained true to his pledge to the end of his noble life. Sometimes in the great audience I would call on him to lead the prayer, and his prayers were like the pleadings of a little child when it had been naughty and the parent was on the point of administering a correction. There were few dry eyes in the house when Grady was praying. He was an efficient officer in the Church and kept near the Master from the time he renewed his vows until that sad, sunny day when, amid a city in mourning and tears, we laid him to rest.

After his death I was asked by a friend: "Who is to take Grady's place?" I replied: "There is no place to take. Grady was a phenomenal man, such as comes on the arena of life once in five hundred years. He brought his place with him, did his work, passed out, and carried his place with him. There is no place for another to take." To which my friend replied: "I believe you are right."

In the most prominent square in his own beloved Atlanta stands his life-sized bronze monument with the inscription: "He literally loved a nation into peace." Peace to his ashes! He will live when monuments have crumbled into dust.

In the midst of my fourth year on this charge the General Conference met in St. Louis, Mo., and I was elected one of the Missionary Secretaries of our Church. Hence I had to surrender my beloved charge after three and a half happy years, having seen more than eight hundred souls converted to God. This closed one of the most successful pastorates ever granted by the Lord of the vineyard to an unworthy laborer. I surrendered the charge, now numbering more than sixteen hundred souls, to my successor, Rev. I. S. Hopkins, D.D., now deceased.

Among the happy memories of those years is my association with Dr. Hawthorne, of the Baptist Church, and Dr. Barnett, of the Presbyterian Church. Our three churches stood in a triangle, and each bore the same given name—"First Church." We were like three brothers, harmoniously working together and helping each other in the Master's work. The other two have gone to the Church triumphant, and I am passing that way while I hold them in loving remembrance.

The close of my work at First Church, Atlanta, also closed my life as a pastor, having served twenty-five years in that capacity and having witnessed more than eight thousand conversions. This, of course, includes the camp meetings and the protracted meetings and work for my fellow pastors, which was very frequent for many years.

CHAPTER VIII.

CONNECTIONAL DUTIES.

> Waft, waft, ye winds, his story,
> And you, ye waters, roll,
> Till, like a sea of glory,
> It spreads from pole to pole. —*Heber*.

At the General Conference of 1890 there were three Missionary Secretaries elected. Dr. I. G. John was the Senior and Office Secretary, and Dr. A. Coke Smith (afterwards bishop) and myself were made Field Secretaries. Before entering upon our work Dr. Smith resigned his office and took another place of service, leaving me alone in the field.

The Board of Missions at its next meeting elected Dr. W. H. Potter, of Georgia, to fill the place made vacant by the resignation of Dr. Smith. Dr. Potter served with me for about a year, when he became ill and almost suddenly died, leaving me again alone in the field.

Dr. W. R. Lambuth (now bishop) had been compelled to leave the mission field in Japan and return home with his wife, whose health was failing. The Board then employed him to take the place made vacant by the death of Dr. Potter. He served but a short time, when the failing health of Dr. John made it necessary for him to leave the field and serve in the office. Thus I was left alone in the field for the third time.

The financial panic of the early nineties caused the Mission Board to become involved in an oppressive debt, reaching at its maximum $172,000. This sum I managed to reduce by the amount of $40,000 while serving in the field.

When the General Conference met at Memphis in 1894, I was made Senior Secretary and had to assume the responsibility of the office at Nashville, Tenn. On reaching the office I found the debt at that time to be $132,000. A foreign missionary debt of this dimension in a period of financial panic was so discouraging that members of the Board believed and said: "To pay this debt is an impossibility." This I knew to be true, unless I could get direction and direct help from God. Hence I said little to any one, but carried the matter direct to him. After a lapse of time, and while kneeling in the secret place, I received the satisfactory consciousness that the debt would be paid. From that hour I was never elated by any unexpected success nor discouraged by any temporary failure. I knew that He who had given assurance would also give direction. Therefore, looking to Him alone and using my best judgment, I proceeded to "follow the cloud."

After arranging matters in the office, I took the field, determined to lay the matter before the men of wealth throughout the bounds of our Methodism, asking for their subscriptions under official guarantee that payment would not be required until the entire debt was pledged. And with this promise I met with success from the beginning.

I traveled through and through the land from Maryland to California. Reaching a city or town, I would generally preach twice on Sunday. Then on

Autobiography of Bishop Henry Clay Morrison.

Monday morning I would get from the pastor the name and residence of such members as were financially able to assist and visit them at once. And here let me say that the gospel is the power of God unto many things other than salvation. The preaching on Sunday gave me a gospel nexus with the people, and when I called the next day I found them accessible and glad of my coming. God **gave** me many a brief love feast with bankers and other business men. I depended on the gospel and the guidance of the Holy Spirit, but never mentioned money from the pulpit.

I pursued this course until $64,000 was pledged, when I conceived the idea of writing a letter to reach those who could pay small amounts and who could not conveniently be seen in person. God directed in this, and after much prayer and thought I formulated that letter so that I would reach both the head and heart. And again I was given divine direction and assurance that the letter would accomplish its purpose. I employed more than sixty women to rewrite that letter *verbatim et literatim et punctuatim*, and they wrote it and rewrote it over forty thousand times. I paid them over $3,000 to do that work, and the letter paid the expense of writing and cleared for the Board over $40,000. This brought the pledges up to $104,000.

Again I took the road, asking for large subscriptions, and did not stop until I reached the sum of $150,000. This gave us a margin of $18,000 over the debt, all of which I collected except a little more than $1,000. This surplus was used by the Board in helping to build three mission churches.

Thus, with the $40,000 raised before I was made Senior Secretary, together with the overplus collected, the entire sum raised was $188,000. This was done in twenty months by following the Hand I could not see. And here I wish to record the fact that those twenty months were the most joyful of my life. There is no joy comparable to that which comes of the consciousness of following "where He leadeth." If I had now the physical strength, I would gladly go again through the travel and toil of the work for the spiritual joy attending it.

In the eight years' service in this office I traveled about twenty times the distance around the earth without one cent of life or accident insurance and never saw a ship in trouble nor a car wheel off the track. I visited and spoke at twenty-one Annual Conferences every year for eight years. With deep gratitude I make this record, feeling that in all my varied experiences beneath me have been the everlasting Arms and above me the Eye that never sleeps.

CHAPTER IX.

The Episcopacy.

> Happy were men if they but understood
> There is no greatness but in doing good.
> —*Fountain.*

In 1898 the General Conference met in Baltimore, Md. Here Dr. W. A. Candler and I were elected to the episcopacy. This office brought new and numerous responsibilities which I felt my inability to meet. But relying on the promise, "Lo, I am with you alway," I entered upon my work.

At my very first Conference I began to observe some things that hitherto in life I had largely overlooked and was brought to see something of the unkindness that an itinerant often receives even from his own people. The Conference was held in a small town, and I was entertained by the pastor of our Church, who was a faithful and successful man. He had succeeded in procuring a new church and parsonage in the three years he had served the charge. But now his energy and efforts had brought his people up to a higher degree of prosperity and respectability, and they wanted a man of more polish for their pulpit and finer social qualities for their parsonage.

The pastor had a son who had recently died of a long-protracted illness. Three physicians attended him, one of whom was a Methodist. Inasmuch as he left nothing for the support of his widow and child except a life insurance policy for a thousand dollars, two of the physicians donated their service, while the Methodist physician made a charge of one hundred and twenty-five dollars. The pastor appealed to him under the circumstances to reduce his bill, whereupon he became offended and said that he would have the pastor removed.

It is astonishing how many things a bishop can find out before he gets to Conference. As usual, I learned these facts in advance. Accordingly, I was invited early in the session to a state dinner with the doctor, who gave his reasons for a change of pastors. I listened, but said nothing. After the dinner I was driven back to the parsonage, and as I stepped from the carriage after reaching the place I said: "Doctor, if your pastor has been guilty of conduct unbecoming a minister of the gospel, you can bring complaints against him and have an investigation of his case." With an expression of mingled disgust and disappointment he drove away, and I never saw him afterwards.

I give this as an illustration of the monumental meanness of some who call themselves Methodists. Alas! "Man's inhumanity to man makes countless thousands mourn."

The General Conference of 1882 was held in Nashville, Tenn. Here I served for the first time as clerical delegate to that body and made my first speech on the floor of a General Conference. That speech was in favor of restricting the term of service in the presiding eldership to four years, making the elder ineligible after serving for that length of time until he had filled other work for a term in the interim. After more than thirty years I still hold the same conviction, and I have generally, though not invariably, carried out this conviction in my official service. This course has often cost severe criticism and misrepresentation, but God has honored the work.

If the proper men are placed in that office and thus restricted in term of service, it will effectually cure the abuses of the office, which have been a source of perpetual discord. This will prevent the formation of "rings" in an Annual Conference, and it will also prevent the suspicion of a ring, which suspicion is often as hurtful as if it had a real foundation. This course, too, will prevent fossilizing by a lifetime incumbency of the office, and it will give to every member of the Conference who has the qualifications to fill the place a chance to serve in that capacity.

Soon after I was placed in the episcopacy there arose a question which threw the Church into fearful discord. An old war claim was collected from the United States government, and the means used for the collection I could not indorse. I differed in kindness from others in this matter and was conscientiously compelled to demur from the final decision of the case. I stood alone, as I shall have to do and am willing to do in the final judgment at the Court of Great Assize.

The duty of raising money for the Church seemed to fall upon me in my early ministry, and I have tried to meet that duty for more than forty years. Whether in the pastorate, secretaryship, or the episcopacy, I have responded to the call of the Church to raise funds for the propagation of her work. Often after preaching, and when a sense of exhaustion bade me sit down, I would open the battle for one, ten, or twenty thousand dollars, holding the people and endeavoring to keep them interested until the amount called for was pledged. On these occasions I have been kept on my feet for three hours and on one occasion for four hours and succeeded in doing what was said to be impossible and which would have been impossible but for divine help. The largest amount I have ever raised in one day was a little more than $75,000. This was the crowning day of my life in this work, never having gone above $26,000 on any other single day.

During the quadrennium which ended at Asheville in 1910 I raised a little more than a quarter of a million dollars, $100,000 of which was secured in the pioneer State of Florida.

During the eighteen years of my service in the episcopacy I have held most of the home Conferences and also those in Mexico and Brazil. I have held some of them as often as four times. I have never served in the Orient. There are fifty-one Annual Conferences at home and abroad, and I have served forty-one of them.

At the General Conference at Asheville, N. C., in 1910 I was unexpectedly waited on by a subcommittee and informed that the Committee on Episcopacy had retired me from office. I went before the committee and was told that complaints had been brought against me. I answered the complaints and was reinstated. Two days later I was again waited on by the same committee and informed that on new complaints I was again retired. I then asked for a committee of investigation to find and investigate what the complaints were against me and report the same to the General Conference, then in session. To this they responded by sending a third committee to inform me that they could not give me a committee of investigation. I asked the reason why they could not give me such a committee. The chairman of the committee replied: "We have nothing to put before a committee of investigation." I asked: "Where are the allegations on which you have twice voted my retirement?" The chairman said: "There are no allegations against you."

Here, then, were three committees, two of them notifying me of my retirement and the third and last committee confessing that there was nothing against me.

Fortunately for me at this juncture, an individual sent in "a charge with specifications." This under the law compels the appointment of a committee of investigation, and but for this I would never have secured such a committee, and the matter would have stood thus: A verdict without charges and specifications, without an investigation, and without notification.

When the Committee of Investigation met and heard the prosecution, the chairman of the committee said: "We are satisfied." He then asked if I wished to introduce any witnesses, to which I replied that I did not. The vote was then taken, which was unanimously in my favor.

Here I wish to say that while passing through this ordeal I felt mortified that I was the center of attraction in the eyes of a curious public. Yet I had no sense of uneasiness. I crept close to the Master and realized his presence and power as never before.

It was a spiritual epoch in my history and the best week of life. Let us but know that we are right with God, and there will be nothing to fear. I record this incident in justice to the Church and my family when I am gone.

The circumstances of this remarkable case have been accurately given by the editor of this book in the following article written at the time and published by many of our Church papers with the indorsement of their editors. The article is as follows:

THE TRIAL OF A BISHOP.

BY REV. G. H. MEANS, IN WESLEYAN CHRISTIAN ADVOCATE.

At the General Conference of 1844, it is a well-known fact, Bishop Andrew was "affectionately requested to resign the office of bishop" on the ground of expediency.

It was not claimed that Bishop Andrew had violated the law. There were no charges against his moral character, no objection to his administration, no claim that he had been guilty of improper conduct, nor that he was worn out and physically unfit for the active duties of the episcopacy.

The whole plea was expediency; that was the text, exordium, argument, and conclusion—expediency.

The Northern delegates rang the changes on this plea in almost every speech. If Bishop Andrew had been unfortunate, he must atone for it. If he had made an honest mistake, it was expedient that he should rectify it by making a more serious one. It was expedient for the majority to wrong the minority; the law was not considered.

Mr. Spencer, of Pittsburgh, voiced the sentiments of the Northern delegates when he said: "Mr. President, how did you and your colleagues get into your episcopal office? Expediency put you there, expediency keeps you there, and when expediency requires it you shall be removed from your seats —yes, every one of you."

Upon this point of expediency turned the whole question of the relation and status of the bishops of the Methodist Episcopal Church. They were regarded by the majority as mere creatures of the General Conference, to be made and unmade at will, subject to the caprices of a body that could remove them with or without cause.

The Southern delegates, representing the slaveholding States, met this onslaught on their constitutional rights by a positive denial. They declared that it was never expedient to violate law, that the bishops were not creatures of the Conference, that the power to make did not involve the power to unmake, and that the bishops were not removable at will without charge or trial. Dr. Lovick Pierce said: "Of all the notions that were ever defended before a body of Christian ministers, the notion of asking an act of this sort on the grounds of expediency, when it was inexpedient for one portion of the united body of Christians to do this, as it is not expedient for the other that it should be done, is to me the most fearful mockery of sound logic. Do that which is inexpedient for us because it is expedient for you! Never while the heavens are above the earth let that be recorded on the journals of the General Conference."

So the question of dealing with our bishops on the grounds of expediency was the entering wedge of separation. This difference regarding the status and relation of bishops exists to-day between the two bodies of Methodism. Only a few years ago several bishops of the Methodist Episcopal Church were relegated to the superannuated ranks on the plea of expediency. Such a thing could not be tolerated in the Methodist Episcopal Church, South. We buried expedience more than half a century ago, never to be resurrected, with the consent of the Church.

But at our late General Conference the Committee on Episcopacy seemed to forget or ignore this historic precedent and proceeded to do, on the ground of expediency, what they could not do by law.

In the case of Bishop Morrison they found two verdicts on the ground of complaints, without written charges and specifications, without a committee of investigation, without notification and in the absence of the accused.

Acting only on the complaints, they voted for the Bishop's retirement without notice and during his absence, although the law says: "A bishop ought to be allowed to be present and to be furnished with a notice when any complaint is about to be preferred against him." (Man. Dis., page 153.)

The Bishop was allowed to come before the committee only after begging for this privilege and after the verdict against him had already been pronounced. Then on the strength of the Bishop's statements the committee reconsidered its action, and he was placed on the effective list.

But a new complaint came in. The case was reopened, and for the second time the Bishop was retired without written charges and specifications and without notification and in his absence. Bishop Morrison then asked for a committee of investigation and was told: "We have nothing to put before it." He then asked for the allegations and was informed: "There is nothing against you." Charges and specifications were later preferred, and a committee of investigation was at last appointed.

But what remained for the Committee of Investigation to do? If the action of the Committee on Episcopacy was legal, the case was settled until it came before the Conference for ratification. If it was not legal, then the two verdicts were of no force. But in either case the committee work had already been done—done on the grounds of complaint, without charges and specifications. The Committee on Episcopacy admitted that it had nothing to put before the Committee of Investigation and that there was nothing against the accused. Nothing against the accused, nothing to put before the Committee of Investigation, and yet two verdicts had been rendered!

But the Committee of Investigation proceeded with the case and found a verdict in the Bishop's favor by unanimous vote. In the meantime the Committee on Episcopacy voted that the complaints against his administration "had been fully sustained." So the two verdicts were at cross purposes. What a medley of legal entanglements and contradictions!

Even the case as brought before the Committee of Investigation was not legal. Bishop Morrison was not furnished with a written copy of charges and specifications until the Conference had assembled and knew nothing of their nature until they were read before the committee.

The law says: "No charge against a bishop shall be tried unless made in writing, with specifications, signed by the accusers, and a copy of the charges and specifications be delivered to the accused a sufficient length of time before the trial to enable him to make all necessary preparations for his defense." (Discipline, paragraph 267.) In Bishop Morrison's case this course was not pursued; no such action was taken. However, he waived this privilege, which gave to the case an appearance of legality, and the case proceeded after it had already been prejudged and prejudiced by a verdict twice rendered and the accused twice notified that his case had been disposed of. All forms of law had been ignored. The Bishop was never called before the Committee on Episcopacy to answer any allegations; no written charges and specifications had been preferred; no proof had been legally taken; no notification had been given; but a verdict had been twice rendered, on the grounds of complaints only, during the absence of the accused.

Now, complaints and charges, as is well known, are not synonyms in Church law. If in our Discipline the terms are sometimes used interchangeably, the context makes the distinction plain. Complaints are not effective unless they are serious enough to be formulated into charges. Character may be arrested on complaints, but before a trial can be projected or a verdict rendered these complaints must take the shape of written charges and specifications. A complaint is not the ground of a trial; it is only preliminary in its nature. It may be a mere grievance that does not affect the character of the administration; it may degenerate into a mere whine of discontent. Complaints may refer only to peccadillos, peculiari-

Autobiography of Bishop Henry Clay Morrison.

ties that are objectionable only to the complainer and that involve no moral obliquity or administrative inefficiency.

Complaints! Who can't complain and growl when a bishop doesn't see through his glasses? At every Annual Conference, and at every session thereof, there are disaffections. Some one is sent where he does not want to go or is kept where he does not want to stay. Some ruling of the bishop or his manner of doing things does not please the minority or perhaps the majority. Can a committee of episcopacy afford to notice these growlings and render a verdict on these grounds? A bishop's rulings may be both lawful and wise and yet be the subject of complaints. Shall these complaints be treated with the same consideration as charges that are required to be supported by proof and that involve the character and conduct of the accused?

What bishop has any protection under such a rule? Charges and specifications have a dignity that commands attention, because they involve the moral character or administrative behavior. But the complaints and murmurings of some chronic grumbler should be ignored. What bishop does not make mistakes? What bishop is there whose acts meet with universal approval? When the time comes that no brother is disgruntled or disappointed, then, and not until then, will complaints cease. And when that time comes look around you for the first glow of the millennial dawn. But as the matter now stands, why should the General Conference play battledore and shuttlecock with their officers for using their judgment in doing the things which the body authorizes them to do? The minority report at the General Conference of 1844 truly said: "Episcopacy is not a mere appointment to labor. The bishops are not the creatures of the General Conference. As executive officers they belong to the Church, and not to the General Conference, as one of its organs of action merely."

If the bishops have too much power, deprive them of it; but don't give them snuff and punish them for sneezing. If they violate the law, try them for it; but don't listen to the whimperings of every little ecclesiastical demiofficial who thinks that all they do ought to meet with his approval. Make him formulate his complaints into charges or else hush his growlings.

Mere complaints may injure one as seriously as charges. Bishop Hedding, on Discipline, says: "The complaint itself, with the statement accompanying it, though a bill may not be found against him, may make impressions on the minds of some that may injure a bishop during life. People ordinarily will not make the distinction between a complaint and a bill, and the mere fact that a bishop is complained of becomes a serious matter."

The law also says: "No person is required to explain or make defense until enough has been proved to warrant a reasonable conclusion against him." In Bishop Morrison's case there were no proofs submitted and no charges legally preferred before the committee that rendered two verdicts against him. If enough had been proved to warrant "a reasonable conclusion against him," he should have been called before a committee to explain or make defense. This was never done; he had access to the committee only by begging this privilege. If enough had not been proved to warrant a reasonable conclusion against him, then the verdict pronounced was not worth the paper on which it was written.

All Church law respecting witnesses and evidence during a trial not only calls for proof, but for an opportunity on the part of the accused to offset such proof, and any verdict in the absence of such provision is null and void.

Dr. Winans, at the General Conference of 1844, struck the keynote of that body's limitations when he said: "A General Conference, in a judicial or other capacity, is bound to proceed by its own laws and to observe its own statutes until they are properly altered, as much so as any inferior judiciary." In other words, the General Conference is not an arbitrary body.

Now, the question is, Did the Committee on Episcopacy intend to observe the law, or did they deliberately ignore it and act on the plea of expediency? No one will claim that the committee did not know the law. It was an intelligent body of men. No one will contend that they were not sincere. Surely they did not allow personal prejudices and interests to influence them in their decisions. They could not have been misled by any complications in the case, because the law is plain. How, then, can we account for the action of the committee except on the grounds of expediency? Did the committee wish to get rid of the Bishop on general principles? Was it with them a question of law or a matter of expediency? And did they adopt the latter and thus go back on our position as a Church, which, since 1844, we have contended for in all our controversies where the relation of the episcopacy has been involved?

It was never claimed at any time that Bishop Morrison had violated the law; and when one of the committee was asked to "put his finger on a single law that he had violated," there was no reply. The Committee on Episcopacy might have been asked to do the same thing with the same result.

What, then, was the offense in the Bishop's case calling for two verdicts retiring him from the active duties of the episcopacy? The "head and front of his offending" was that he was "inefficient and unacceptable in his administration." Now, if he had violated no law, he had only exercised his judgment in the application of the law and in doing so had displeased certain parties. In one instance it was stated that he had "become mentally incapacitated to discharge his duties as a bishop," a very natural conclusion with some persons when others run counter to their views. He had done just what the Church had authorized him to do, but his manner of doing it did not please everybody.

Now, the Church invests the bishops with certain powers. Why should they be called to account for doing what they are authorized to do? The minority report in that memorable Conference of 1844 voiced the sentiment of the Methodist Episcopal Church, South, when it said: "When a bishop is suspended or is informed that it is the wish of the General Conference that he cease to perform the functions of a bishop for doing what the law of the same body allows him to do, then the whole procedure becomes an outrage upon justice as well as upon law."

That is the case, *multum in parvo*. Authorize the bishop to do a thing and punish him for doing it! Invest a bishop with certain powers and humiliate him for exercising them! How can any bishop know his legal whereabouts when he is tossed on the wave of every opinion and is subject to every whim?

Bishop Soule said in 1844: "The Church has made special provision for the trial of a bishop, for the special reason that a bishop has no appeal."

Therefore, as the bishop cannot appeal his case, his trial should be careful and complete. The witnesses should be unimpeachable; neither should there be chronic grumblers and complainers. The evidence should be positive and not mere opinions based on grievances. The charges and specifications should involve moral character and maladministration and not mere peccadillos. The administration should be judged by the law and not by the little accidents involved in the case. Due notice should be given the accused, and he should be allowed to be present. The verdict is final, and anything like carelessness or precipitation is illegal, cruel, and unjust.

Now to sum up the facts in Bishop Morrison's case: First, he was tried on complaints without written charges and specifications. It matters not what the complaints were; complaints are not the grounds of the trial. Second, he was tried during his absence without any sort of notification and without his knowledge. Third, he was never at any time called before the Committee on Episcopacy and was admitted to that body only by begging permission to appear before it. Fourth, he was retired twice by vote before a committee of investigation was appointed in his case. Fifth, the Committee of Investigation was appointed after it was admitted that they "had nothing to put before it" and that there was nothing against him. Sixth, the Committee of Investigation found a verdict in the Bishop's favor, and simultaneously the Committee on Episcopacy rendered a verdict against him.

If this is law, we would better revise our code of practice. If it is not law, it comes from a dangerous source as a precedent for the Church and ministry. Even the complaints on which the Bishop was retired by the Committee on Episcopacy were so frivolous and baseless that the Committee of Investigation, after hearing them, did not think it necessary for the Bishop to introduce his witnesses. Many of these individual complaints were offset by committees and resolutions coming up from the very Conferences where they originated. And in not a single case was it shown that it was the voice of any Conference that the Bishop would be unacceptable should he be returned to preside over their deliberations.

It is a source of satisfaction that the committee were not a unit on any question connected with Bishop Morrison's case. Whether they differed on questions of law or expediency or both, it is not worth while to inquire; they evidently did not agree on doing a wrong to one of the most faithful and effective servants of the Church. And be it said to the credit of a part of that committee that no man ever had stancher friends than those who stood by the Bishop in the most trying hour of his life. This case will go down in history as the most unique that ever agitated a Christian body.

The cases of Bishops Andrew and Morrison are almost parallel, inasmuch as neither was accused of immorality or maladministration, and neither was worn out and physically unfitted for the active duties of the episcopacy. It was no more lawful to superannuate the one than to depose the other. But expediency evidently played its part in both cases. The apostle says: "All things are lawful unto me, but all things are not expedient." Our verdict too often is: "All things are expedient unto me, but all things are not lawful." It is never expedient to do an unlawful thing; and as we many years ago on this very subject repudiated expediency, there is no reason why we should indorse it now.

I have written up this case that the Church may get the facts which are due to the Church and which have never yet been fully published in any form. I have written for the Church on the plain surface facts of the law, that the Church may be informed concerning this matter. Bishop Morrison is an officer of the Church, and the Church ought to know what has been done. The Bishop did not instigate this article, nor did he even remotely suggest it; but the Church is entitled to it, even though the Bishop should not indorse it.

I have served six years since the occurrence recorded above; and if it be the will of God that I live and serve for two years longer, until the General Conference of 1818, I shall with gratitude and gladness ask to be allowed to retire from active official service. I lay my official armor down with the kindest of feeling toward all men and gratitude to God for mercies untold. If God should grant me two more years of service, I will have closed fifty-five years of labor in the ministry. They have been happy years, but filled with incessant toil; but

> "Had we a thousand lives to give,
> Lord, they should all be thine."

I know that the evening shadows are lengthening, but "at the evening time it is light." Every glittering star is jeweled with a joy, and some of my fondest earthly hopes that perished in their bloom will erelong be changed to an eternal fruition. When I lay aside my ministerial robes, I shall sadly miss many delightful and sacred associations with my brethren. But the ties of friendship will not be broken. Its golden links, welded by the eternal Hand, will reunite our souls in that land into whose splendors there comes no parting and no night.

CONCLUSION.

BY THE EDITOR.

> How calmly sinks the setting sun!
> While twilight lingers still,
> Beautiful as a dream of heaven
> It slumbers on the hill.   —*Prentice.*

WHATEVER may be said about the value of an autobiography, its chief charm lies in its candor and simplicity. We want to feel that it is true, formed and fashioned fresh from nature's hand. In the present instance we have the plain, unadorned story of an active life. There is no self-laudation, no boasting of achievements, and no striving after dramatic effect. The story flows on o'er crag and moor, and we follow on as its simple music sings its way into our hearts.

The author lays no claim to fame, although much that he has told us will live in future years. He hides no faults, but comes with self-accusing grief and lays them before us with the lessons they teach—lessons that flash like signal lights over the storm-tossed sea. If as a son he had stressed his devotion to his parents, if as a citizen he had emphasized his defense of the right, if as a soldier he had boasted of his courage, if as a pastor he had advertised his faithfulness, or if as an officer in the higher ranks of ministerial life he had trumpeted his achievements, the story would have defeated its own end. But we look in vain for one glimpse of the ego, one self-assertive declaration of superior merit, or one dogmatic claim of infallible judgment. There is no rancor concealed in his heart toward those who have differed from him, and he indulges in no vituperation toward those who have tried to injure him.

These facts will accrue to the author's credit all the more when we remember that Kentucky nature is impetuous, self-willed, and too often obstinate and defiant. While it is true to its convictions, dauntless in danger, and never raises the white flag on the fields of conflict, yet it requires much grace to direct its energies aright and hold them in line.

A few incidents from the author's own pen reveal the fact that his blood is hot. It reveals the taint of a temper which, if the grace of God had not restrained, would have left on his garments the stain of blood. But haply he escaped to tell the story of deliverance as an object lesson to others.

From the time Moses slew the Egyptian and Jesus said to the impulsive Peter, "Put up thy sword," until now no one has figured in the annals of the Church more dynamic even to rashness than Martin Luther. But all his impetuous nature was consecrated to God and the cause he espoused. If Luther had been as tame and fearful as Melanchthon or as gentle and unoffending as Zwingli, the Reformation would be but the memory of a fatal failure. The battle of the Reformation was won by the dogged determination of the man who said: "I would go to Worms if every tile on the housetop were a devil." Such unswerving and uncompromising spirits have always been in the vanguard of victory, with the seal of God's sanction on their souls. The rarest of all Christian virtues is boldness, and it is one of the greatest assets of a soldier of the cross.

I am not apologizing for the character of the author; it has never been attacked and needs no defense. Even those who differed from him most bitterly never tinged their arrows with the poison of vituperation or suspicion. Nor am I apologizing for his traits. Some of the most useful of God's servants have been reservoirs of unspent thunder, and God never apologized for their impetuous natures while he directed their energies.

It cannot be denied that the Bishop's usefulness in some respects is without a parallel in the annals of Southern Methodism. The Church has had but few men in the episcopacy who have stood out prominently as solicitors of funds, and even those few have no such record as Bishop Morrison. More than three millions of dollars have been poured into the treasury of the Church by his hand, and in this respect he is without a peer in the history of our Zion. But great as this work is and has been, it is not the most vital. Orthodox to the core, he has had no patience with the "Advanced Thought," "New Thought," "Science," falsely so called, and all the other fads, fancies, and follies that have cursed the Church in latter years. Converted by the grace of God to the old-time religion in the old-time way, he has championed the old-time methods and held the Church to the old landmarks.

I would not be understood as recording the virtues of the Bishop. Perhaps no one has been closer to him than the editor of this work. I have known of his pastoral career, having been stationed in the same city, and on one occasion succeeded him in the pastorate. I have known him in his home life, in his charities and friendships, his afflictions, bereavements, in all the sad, sacred, and varied relations of life, and from personal knowledge I can confidently assure all who read this book that the religion he has so earnestly preached to others he has most assiduously enjoyed and practiced himself. And to every young preacher it will be an inspiration to know that the duties of the ministry he enjoins upon them he has observed to the limit of his ability. But I forbear, lest I be accused of indulging in a fulsome eulogy prompted by the sympathies of friendship.

On the Bishop's character and traits I have only touched at a tangent, preferring to present the life as a whole instead of delineating specific traits. The charm of the rainbow lies in its reflecting all the tints of nature, and human character shines best when all its virtues are solidified.

A minister, whether in the pastorate or episcopacy, cannot be judged by isolated acts of administration. Nor can he be justly judged by acts that have within them the principle of continuity unless the motives that actuated them are known and the facts are marshaled before us, with all their intricate bearings upon the cases in question. Then a just judgment may or may not be rendered, because partiality or prejudice may warp the verdict.

Who knows what a pastor's secret difficulties are in dealing with questions pertaining to his flock? They are never heralded to the world. Who knows what a bishop's problems are in adjusting matters that pertain to his duties, whose far-reaching consequences affect, not a single congregation only, but many places and pastors, all of which must be conserved? The facts in full are seldom, if ever, revealed.

If a bishop's administration were local, then local wants might be supplied and local factions satisfied. But as it is, the most painstaking work may cause some to smile while others weep, and some one is sure to get the praise or blame.

I write this not in defense of the subject of this sketch, but in the interest of the episcopal office. Until we know all the facts, with all their entangling ramifications, we would better heed the Scriptural injunction: "Obey them that have the rule over you, and submit yourselves: for they watch for your souls, as they that must give an account, that they may do it with joy, and not with grief: for that is unprofitable for you."

No bishop will claim that he has not made mistakes in his administration, and it is not the province of his dearest friend to apologize for his errors. Let them float down the tide with the flotsam and jetsam of life until they enter the sea without a shore.

The life of Bishop Morrison is before us from the budding of springtime until the autumn leaves grow purple on the hills. And now that the winter is passed and the summer ended, in the mellow ripeness of age, with a consciousness of duty done, he is ready to lay the garnered sheaves at the Master's feet. His children, honored and loved, are settled around him. A few have passed over and up. Not many years ago a son in the full flush of a noble manhood was called above. In a letter to this editor is the father's account of the son's last hours. Dickens's "Death of Little Nell" is not more beautifully pathetic than this threnody of a father's sorrowing heart. The letter reads:

ATLANTA, GA., January 16, 1902.

Dear Brother Means: Your beautiful letter did us good in our grief. We have had all that friends could give. We also have the blessing of God in the full assurance that the dear boy was ready to go.

His going was as beautiful as it was sudden and unexpected. Five minutes before he was gone we did not think him dangerously ill. It was paralysis of the heart.

He came and met us at this place and spent the Christmas with us. The day after he arrived he asked to have a private talk with me. He said: "I want to tell you all about my life and experience since I have been away at school. I have had doubts and hard battles. Sometimes I have had terrible temptations. I would be less than a man to receive your kindness and then keep anything from you. I want you to know my heart fully and all my inner life."

After talking for a while he said: "I have now told you all, and it is a relief to know that you know my heart perfectly. But I am not satisfied with my religious experience. I want the peace of which you have so often told me." I said it was his privilege to have this peace and that I was praying for him daily. Raising his eyes to mine, he said: "Will you pray for me now?" We kneeled together, and as we prayed he entered into a great struggle of soul. We lingered for a time, then, arising from his knees, he threw his arms about my neck and said: "The burden is all gone now. I have perfect peace, and I will now try to do whatever God wants me to do if I can find out what it is. I want to pray now." So we bowed together, and he led the prayer, thanking God for his goodness and for the sweet peace he had given him.

The second morning following he led the family devotions as if he had been long used to that duty. Two days after this he went to bed with a deep cold, but did not seem to be seriously ill, and the morning of his death he seemed to improve slowly and sat up for an hour in bed. After breakfast he said: "I feel better and will soon be able to return to school." About noon he complained that he could not breathe and in five minutes was in the spirit world.

My fondest earthly hope has perished. But God knows best. His will be done. I shall meet my boy again.

Without the Bishop's knowledge I give this tint in the picture of his home life, because it has its lesson and tells its own story. The gospel which he had so faithfully preached to others was his consolation now, the faith which he had so earnestly enjoined transmuted his grief into peace, and as the clouds of sorrow grew luminous with the dawn of heaven he could say: "I shall meet my boy again." This boy, whom the father fondly hoped would sometime become a herald of the cross, in life's morning went up the shining way into a broader field. To the father's faith he is not dead; only God's finger touched him, and he slept.

The Bishop's faithful companion is with him yet. Her face still glows with "a light that ne'er was seen on land or sea." Together they have climbed many a hill of difficulty, crossed many deserts where the sands were hot, drank deeply at Siloam's fountain, and tasted the waters of Marah, that lay black and bitter in their pools. They have come from night to light, through pain to peace, and happy and hopeful they now stand upon the banks of the mystic river that flows on without a discordant note of song.

> "O the blessèd hope of immortality! It o'ersweeps
> All pains, all tears, all time, all fears, and peals
> Like the eternal thunders of the deep
> Into my ears this truth: thou livest forevermore."

APPENDIX.

REMINISCENCES AND REFLECTIONS.

> Our memory brightens o'er the past,
> As when the sun, concealed
> Behind some cloud that near us hangs.
> Shines on a distant field. —*Longfellow.*

IN writing the story of my life I do not claim to have contributed anything new or startling to the history or literature of the day. It is the simple story of my life unembellished by literary excellence and untarnished by sensational narrations. I have written to preserve a record of my life for the benefit of my family and friends and those who may feel an interest in my humble and uneventful career. My purpose is to leave a record that will do good when I am gone; that will warn the erring of unseen dangers or inspire some struggling soul on life's rough road. If in any sense or to any extent this end has been gained, I shall not have written in vain.

So in this chapter of "Reminiscences and Reflections" I would add a few observations for the benefit of young preachers, whose path, though pleasant, has its pitfalls and who may profit by the experience of one who has trudged along the way.

1. *Always depend on divine aid.* Among the many things that fill my heart with gratitude is the clearness and instantaneousness of divine direction given at the important epochs in life. My conversion was instan-

taneous and beyond question. A like instantaneous impression led me into the ministry. The call came to me as unexpectedly as a thunderbolt out of a cloudless sky, but from that hour to this I have never doubted that the call was the voice of God.

It was an instantaneous impression, too, that led me to go into the Confederate army. I was spending the night with an aged couple, and in the evening twilight I walked to the woods and was kneeling in prayer when the impression came with convincing force, "Go to the army." The next morning, heeding the call, I left the circuit of which I had charge, never to return. If in the past God had called his servants to arms in defense of their country, it should not be thought strange that in later times he should call them to minister to men and point them to heaven from the bloody fields of battle.

So I repeat: Follow divine impressions; only be sure they are divine impressions and not human inclinations.

2. *Never lose faith in the supernatural.* While we do not credit the visions and so-called revelations claimed by fanatics, yet we are sure that we are often in closer touch with the Unseen than we are aware. And I regret the efforts of some in modern times who would eliminate the supernatural from the Bible. Do this, and the Bible will mean no more than any other book on history and morals.

There are no doubt premonitions arising out of physical conditions or mental unsoundness that should be ignored, yet not all can be classed as delusions, as the Bible and human experience abundantly prove.

Autobiography of Bishop Henry Clay Morrison.

In my early ministry, when on a circuit more than a hundred miles from home and with an appointment to preach the next day, I received an impression during the night to go home. There was no railroad, and the only mode of travel was on horseback, which required a two days' journey. I had seen no vision, heard no voice, nor had I dreamed; but the impression possessed me, and I could not shake it off. It said: "Go home." It was embarrassing. The family with whom I stopped was going to church to hear me preach, and I could not explain to them my state of mind. But with as few words as possible I bade them farewell and, mounting my horse, took my journey homeward. I arrived in the night on the evening of the second day, and when I went into my father's room I found him in a dying condition and unable to speak to me. From whence came that impression? There was no telegraph, no telephone, and no other mode of communication to call me home.

So I hold that we should not always ignore such intimations of duty, even in matters of a similar kind.

3. *Pray in the common affairs of life.* An incident of this necessity entered into my experience which will ever be remembered. It was during the war, when bands of armed marauders infested the country under the name of home guards and made it hazardous to travel the public highways.

Our neighborhood was separated from the adjoining one by a deep, sluggish, muddy creek, with abrupt banks and low bottoms on each side. It was perhaps two miles or more between the highlands on each side. Being on the opposite side from my home on one occasion, I undertook to cross the wide bottoms in the nighttime to reach my home. I was riding a horse that knew nothing of the bridle path that crossed the bottom. The night was dark, and the dense forest made the darkness like that of Egypt. I had just entered the forest when my animal became frightened, shied, and lost the path. I dismounted and tried to find the path by feeling along the ground, but all in vain. I was lost, and I knew that if I ever saw the loved ones at home again I must get to them before daylight, as it was almost certain death to be seen in the daytime.

But the path could not be found, and, accepting the situation, with my saddle for a pillow, I lay down and tried to sleep. But the cry of the night birds, the hooting of owls, together with the sense of danger, drove sleep from my eyes and produced a feeling of loneliness and unrest that cannot be described. I arose, saddled my horse, and knelt before God in prayer. I prayed with that sense of helplessness to which he lends a listening ear. When I arose from my knees, I again began to search for the lost path, which I found in a few moments, and soon reached my home in safety.

And so I insist that even in the common affairs of life "commit thy way unto the Lord, trust also in him, and he shall bring it to pass."

4. *Have the courage of your convictions.* Let no fear of foes, favor of friends, nor even the bonds of human obligation swerve you from the path of right. In this you will be tried as perhaps you will in no other way. Every man must decide, soon or late, for

God or man in life's emergencies, and "to his own master he standeth or falleth."

I have met many such entanglements in my experience. But one illustration will suffice. In the summer before the close of the Civil War one Captain K——, a hot-blooded Irishman, was sent with a company into Western Kentucky on a recruiting expedition. I knew the Captain, had his confidence, and took the opportunity of going with him on a little visit to the loved ones at home. A number of men who had served out the term for which they volunteered were not permitted to return to their homes, but took the liberty of going without leave. Captain K—— determined to take those men back to the army and deceived them with the promise that a "full amnesty" would be granted them if they would return, although they were kept under guard on their way back.

Among the number was one John J——, a splendid specimen of manhood, handsome, magnetic, and influential with his comrades. He did not feel safe in returning South. As I had the confidence of the Captain, I could ride and talk with liberty to any of the men. Riding beside John J——, he said in a low tone: "If you find out that it is not safe for me to go back, let me know it at once."

I made the promise, and that afternoon, while riding with the Captain, he became quite confidential and said with an oath: "I am going to have John J—— court-martialed and shot as soon as we reach headquarters. He is to blame for all those men leaving the army."

As the evening wore on I fell back by the side of

Autobiography of Bishop Henry Clay Morrison.

John J——; and when he asked me if I had found out anything, I replied: "I found out enough to say that I do not want to see you go much farther South." He turned deathly pale, but made no reply. That night he knocked down his guard, escaped to the woods, and the next time we heard from him he was safe in the State of Illinois.

I knew full well the awful risk I took, but under the circumstances I could see no gain to come to the Confederacy to shoot that young man down like a beef. So I took the risk, saved him from such a doom, and have never regretted the action.

5. *Meet infidelity on its own chosen field.* Flail the monster with its own weapons. Show the folly and danger of unbelief by admitted facts that appeal to human conscience and the import of which is easily comprehended. This was Paul's method, and we are not likely to improve on it.

While pastor in Louisville, Ky., there came a call for a sermon at the Northwestern Agricultural Fair in Peoria, Ill. The fair was to hold for two weeks, and they wished the sermon on the intervening Sunday at two o'clock in the afternoon. I accepted the call and reached the city on the Friday preceding the services and was placed at Ingersoll's old clubhouse for entertainment, the place where the "Colonel" wrote the "Mistakes of Moses" and other infidel productions.

The city was flourishing, with perhaps fourteen whisky distilleries and beer breweries and other industries in proportion. It was a merry multitude that gathered at that clubhouse, chiefly young men, with a few of riper years who were leaders. They seemed to have wealth, intelligence, culture, refinement, and everything but God; they had left God out of their curriculum. They had a certain pride in Mr. Ingersoll as a man of national reputation, and yet they did not fully indorse his ideas and teaching. They would gather in the hotel parlor in the evening after tea, ask questions concerning Christ, the Scriptures, and the Christian system, continuing this until the late hours. I had a peculiar readiness in answering those questions that I had never before experienced, a divine help from Him whose promise cannot fail.

The Sabbath came, and the multitudes assembled at the Fair Grounds for the service. Quite a number of preachers were present, but not one would consent to go with me up on the platform. I never knew the reason for their refusal, unless it was a latent fear of a Rebel from the South.

The Secretary of the Association, Major W———, was a courteous gentleman, and with him seated on my right and a Jewish rabbi on my left, a band of musicians at my feet, the United States flag above my head, and four thousand people in the amphitheater before me, I opened the service. The subject was "Soul-Building," and the text was: "I commend you to God and the word of his grace, which is able to build you up," etc. The audience was attentive and frequently demonstrative in appreciation.

During the discourse I was led to touch up the views of the Secretary, who was a Darwinian. I remarked: "Our evolution friends"—and the Major turned nervously in his seat—"have managed to build up a fine world from what they are pleased to call 'the lower form of matter.' It is a fine piece of work. I see broad prairies, fine stock, splendid men, and elegant ladies—a magnificent piece of work. But they are like the Chinese, who are said to have been three hundred years trying to make a barrel. They finally succeeded in making the barrel with the help of a man inside of it; but how to get the man out was a problem they never could solve. So the evolutionists have built up a fine world from the 'lower form of matter'; but just where that lower form of matter came from they have never been able to tell." This was received with vociferous cheering.

Knowing, as I did, the Ingersollic atmosphere of the surroundings, I took occasion to say: "We know with certainty of three, and only three, inhabited worlds—heaven, earth, and hell. We infer that some of the planets are inhabited, but this is only inference; it is not a demonstrated fact. This little intermediate planet we call earth is the only world that has an infidel in it. There is not an infidel in heaven nor in hell. Those in heaven know the truth of Christianity by its fortunate acceptance; those in hell know its truth by the awful consequences of its rejection. A man may start to hell an infidel, but he gets there a believer and sends back the warning to others that 'they come not into this place of torment.'" I spoke for an hour with that liberty which only the Holy Spirit can give and closed the discourse amid shouts from the audience: "Go on, go on!"

During a ministry of fifty years I have seldom felt the divine help more forcibly and sensibly than on that afternoon, and I have the humble hope of meeting some in the final day who were brought nearer to Christ at that hour.

6. *Do not deviate from the path of duty.* Many alluring inducements will come to you, but let the conviction of duty have the right of way in your life.

During my pastorate in Louisville, Ky., I had a visit from my long-time and special friend, Rev. David Morton. D.D., of Russellville, Ky., who afterwards became known and renowned as the first Secretary of the Board of Church Extension of the Methodist Episcopal Church, South. At the proper time and in a formal manner he proceeded to lay before me the object of his visit. He said: "I am sent at the request of the Board of Trustees of the Logan Female College to inform you that by a unanimous vote of that Board you have been elected to the presidency of the college. And they have commissioned me to inform you and insist that you accept the position. It is, as you know, an important and valuable institution to the Methodism of the State and the only college we have within the bounds of the Louisville Conference. The Board is very anxious that you accept this place of honor and responsibility."

When he had finished his presentation speech I replied: "Please say to the members of your Board that I deeply appreciate their confidence and the compliment implied in their action, but tell them that a number of years since I received a commission from a higher source to preach the gospel, and when that commission is rescinded and I receive from the same source a commission as college president I shall be ready to serve them."

A half-indignant look of disappointment came over the good man's face, and he said with seeming impatience: "Morrison, you never did have common sense." To which I replied: "I know that. Please tell me something that I do not already know."

I give this incident not to discourage others from entering that field of labor if their conscience approves, but to me no other line of endeavor ever appealed that would lead me from my commission.

7. Be true to the homes of the people. Cullen B—— was a farmer in West Tennessee. He was not wealthy, but was in comfortable circumstances. He had a good home, with a nice, well-kept farm, a devoted wife, and two small children about four and six years of age. A party of soldiers came to his home and conscripted him into the army, extorting a promise that he would report in due time. By what authority this was done, he never knew.

En route to the army I spent the night in his home, and he arranged to go with me the next day. The morning came, and his good wife prepared an early breakfast, which was set by the light of a candle. He was sad and silent. The wife and mother seemed paralyzed with inexpressible grief. The little ones, aroused all too early and placed at the table, looked first at the father and mother and then at the stranger as if they were dazed and wondering what it all meant. I took my breakfast with little relish, while their effort to eat was but a courteous pretense. Altogether I have faced few sadder scenes than at that breakfast table.

I could not witness the parting. So, after finishing the meal, I went immediately to the stable, saddled my horse, and awaited his coming. Perhaps it was disloyalty or lack of patriotism; be it so, I spoke from the heart and said to him when he came: "Your first duty is to that heartbroken wife and those little ones, too young to know their loss. Take my advice: unsaddle that horse and go back and take care of your family. The war is about at an end, and you can do no good by going, and I do not believe that God requires it of you. You did not volunteer, therefore your honor is not at stake."

"No," he said quietly, "I promised to go, and I am going." He went, but never returned. A wound received in his first engagement resulted in his death.

8. *Let no one despair of mercy and salvation.* It was in Louisville, Ky., and late in November. The day was chilly, and the atmosphere had a penetration from which one shrank as if every spot on the person were a nerve center. It was a day when one wished to draw up in a comfortable corner and be let alone.

I was in the midst of a protracted meeting, and at the close of an afternoon service as I was leaving the church a messenger came, saying: "There is a woman very ill in Portland who wishes to see you." I asked the name, which was strange to me. It was four miles to Portland, and the car was a horse car heated by a monkey stove. There were ministers living near her, and I asked why she did not send for a minister who lived near by. The reply was: "She said somehow she felt that if she could see you you could tell her what to do."

Autobiography of Bishop Henry Clay Morrison.

The day was waning, the trip long, and I was weary; but there was only one thing to do. Entering the street car and drawing myself up in a corner, I sat mute and chill through the long ride. Reaching the door of her cottage, I was admitted by an elderly woman. The curtains were drawn, and the darkness in the room made it difficult for some moments to take in the surroundings. Gradually I was enabled to see some one on a bed in one corner of the room and a little boy of perhaps seven years. The sick woman appeared to be about fifty years of age, with emaciated features and an anxious facial expression that indicated the near approach of death. After introducing myself, she said: "I never saw you before, but I have heard of you, and I felt that if I could only see you you might tell me what to do. I was at one time a Christian, but in the cares and hardships of life I neglected my duties, and now I am not prepared to die. I have been so unworthy and neglectful that I fear I can never again have the peace that I once had."

I said nothing for a time, but permitted her without interruption to indulge in those self-criminations. Then I said: "Sister, you can never change what is past. But Christ will forgive all that. Quit thinking of yourself. It will do you no good. Turn your thoughts away from yourself and your past and fix them upon Christ, who loved you and gave himself for you and who loves you now." After quoting his promises and singing a verse or two, we knelt in prayer, while the little boy came and knelt close by me. While we prayed a change came, the room seemed to grow brighter, and I heard a low, soft voice saying, "Bless the Lord." It seemed as if earth and heaven were coming together in that humble cottage. As we arose from prayer, with a heavenly brightness on her wan face she said: "I can die now. It is all well. Glory, glory!"

I have never known who received the greater blessing, that poor dying woman or myself. I was not an hour in that cottage, but I went home with a song in my heart, while the very air seemed to have changed and become pleasant. I never saw that poor woman again. She passed to the other life, and we may meet again where we will be as the angels of God.

9. *Finally, "fear God and keep his commandments."* There is much that must be left unsaid. But to sum up:

Be a gentleman, a Christian gentleman, in the home, in the social circle, and in all the relations of life.

Observe the unwritten ethics of the ministry; treat your brothers with courtesy. When you leave a work by the law of limitation or for any other reason, leave it to God and your successor, and do not offend the one nor embarrass the other by interfering with their work.

Be true to the doctrines of the Church. If you cannot conscientiously preach the doctrines of Methodism, leave her pales. Do not eat her bread and smite the hand that feeds you.

Be kind, but firm, and let not the good you do or try to do "be evil spoken of."

Now, in giving this advice I am aware of the fact that I have told you nothing new, nothing that you did not already know; but my object has been to stir up your pure minds by way of remembrance. Neither do I set myself up as an example. I do not claim to be a paragon of perfection. But if I have had any success in the ministry of our Lord, I owe it under God to the fact that I have tried to live the life that in my declining years I recommend to you.

My whole earthly career seems a strange romance. I cannot understand it. There can be but one explanation: God has directed it. I had but few early advantages, with never a day at college. Without health and battling for life during most of my youth—three times given up to die—I now find myself, at the age of seventy-five years and in the fifty-third year of my ministry, in good health and with strength to meet the duties assigned me by the Church.

My life and its work have been imperfect, but it has pleased the Master to use me, I trust, to some purpose. He can make our weakness the background of his power. Unto him be the honor and the glory now and forever.

GOSPEL TALKS.

> First I would have thee cherish truth
>   As leading star in virtue's train;
> Folly may pass, nor tarnish youth,
>   But falsehood leaves a poison stain.
>
> —*Eliza Cook.*

THE EAGLE'S NEST.

Text: "As an eagle stirreth up her nest, fluttereth over her young, spreadeth abroad her wings, taketh them, beareth them on her wings: so the Lord alone did lead him." (Deut. xxxii. 11, 12.)

God puts his relation to us under the strongest metaphors. He is our Sun, our Munition of rocks; he is for us the Lion of the tribe of Judah, and his care for us like that of the eagle caring for its young.

This king of the air, whose habitat is on high and whose loyalty is universal, is here made to illustrate God's care over his people. It has its home and brings its young into life amid the inaccessible cliffs at the highest point possible above the earth, with the constant aim to teach and train them for a still higher element. The eagle lives apart from the earth and has as little as possible to do with it and is most at home when beyond the clouds.

This World Is the Eyrie of Souls.

This is God's principal use for this world, to make of it a nursery in which to rear his young. The harmonious process of the seasons, the bloom and blight of the flowers, the growth and decay of the fruits, and the alternation of daylight and darkness—all the processes of the universe are incidental to this. They are simply relative, shading into the one grand design of preparing souls for the future state.

When this aim is accomplished and the last of the immortal eaglets have fledged and flown, then the old nest shall be burned up. "The earth shall melt with fervent heat."

The Mission of the Holy Spirit.

This is to bring dead souls to life and then nurture and lead them into all truth. This process of divine incubation is alone the work of the Holy Spirit. "You hath he quickened who were dead in trespasses and in sins." As the eaglet comes into life on the summit of the cliff, as far removed as possible from the earth, so the soul when born of God is at a point of separation from the world. Just where the soul reaches the world's upper and outer verge, where it puts the world underfoot, there it comes into life and is born of God. Then begins that process of education and development for those higher and eternal realms where it is to live with God and where duration is measured only by the clock of eternity.

"Fluttereth Over Her Young."

This Hebrew word "flutter" bears likeness to that in Genesis, first chapter: "The Spirit of God moved [or brooded] upon the face of the waters." That word implies the peculiar tremulous motion of the parent bird when fostering its young, imparting to them life and warmth. The life of the soul, like that of the fledgling, depends on this brooding and fostering of the Holy Spirit. The Holy Ghost must not only quicken us into life, but there must be a continuous fostering and communication of life to us.

How we hang upon the divine motherhood, as dependent as the birdling that waits and lifts its head to receive what the mother bird may bring! We wait at night until he sends slumber to the eyelids. We wait at morning until he sends light to the eyes. We wait until, by a beneficent heaven and a productive earth, he sends our food and raiment. Helpless, immortal fledglings, requiring a whole lifetime to get us ready to fly!

How Fortunate That the Spirit Abides with Us!

So numerous and deadly are the enemies of the soul that death is the result should the Divine Spirit be taken from us. The partridge of the field and the vulture of the air reach a point where they are self-sustaining and self-depending, where they depend no longer upon parental fostering. But we never get strong enough to live and walk without the help of the Holy Spirit. Hence he abides with us, holds us by the hand, leads us, so that when we fall we are not "utterly cast down." Herein is our safety; not in our own, but in the divine strength.

A gentleman and his wife, with their little son, were ascending the Alps on a tour. The father and child were in advance. The mother, anxious about her darling, called to him: "Willie, have you fast hold of your father's hand?" "No, mamma," said the child: "but father has fast hold of my hand." Here is safety:

not in our grasp upon God, but in his grasp upon us. We are safe just as long as we are willing for him to hold us by the hand and lead us. But the danger lies in our peevish and rebellious hours, when we try to pull loose from the divine grasp and have our own way.

"Stirreth Up Her Nest."

This prowess of dealing with its young is remarkable. Fed to fullness and stupidity, the birdlings lie in their nest in a state of inactivity and make no effort to try their powers or prepare for flight until the parent bird begins to stir up the nest and box them about and make it uncomfortable for them to remain in that state. Here we have a picture of God's providential efforts to develop and educate us. The overfed fledgling is not more at ease in the nest than men are in this world when every want is met. And could we but have things as we wish and perpetuate that state, too many would be willing to remain thus and never aspire to a higher being.

Take it, as a rule, where you find affluence and ease, you find the least desire and effort for a holy life. Where there is most prosperity, there is generally least piety. Where there is temporal fullness, there is little "panting after God." Human nature is stupid and earthy. Fill it with temporal good, and it is willing to luxuriate, sleep, and dream, and has small care for a higher being.

God Has to Keep Us Stirred Up.

We have to be boxed and beaten into willingness to rise above mere earthly ease and comfort. Fifty years ago this Southland was asleep in the lap of luxury. But we did not sleep very long until we were stirred up by the war spirit, and so fearful was the stirring that many were willing to leave their own land and seek refuge and rest in other countries. There was an absolute revolution. Poverty and leanness stalked through the land like the "lean kine" from the sea. The fatness and wealth went from the face of the country, and the very customs and styles were largely changed, while the Old South is to-day a sentimental memory. Take the history of the nations, and you find the hand of God about them in the periodical stirrings which have marked their march down the ages.

He deals with the family as with the nation. How often he stirs up the home circle! I see them daily discomfited by misfortune, disease, and death. I see a Christian home in dangerous ease and luxury, blessings on every hand, but there is forgetfulness of God —no home altar, no thanksgiving, no recognition of God, spiritually asleep in the home nest. The eagle may forget her young, but God will not forget that home. He strikes that home with a wing stroke of his providence that shocks it into life and activity. A darling daughter, noble son, or loving parent falls dangerously ill. Solicitude fills that home. A sense of helplessness brings them to think of God and to call him to their help, whom they had well-nigh forgotten. Perchance the stroke is fatal; remedies fail; the death angel enters, the grim casket receives its dead, and the slow-moving procession turns from that stricken home to "the home of all the living." How many homes wherein God was forgotten have had thought and life turned toward the sky by these wing strokes of the divine Parent!

We Understand Only One Side.

We can easily understand the fostering, the feeding, and the warning processes. It is no miracle to us when he brings us a tidbit of good fortune or luscious piece of good luck. How we chuckle and smile and enjoy it! I never knew any one puzzled in regard to the palatable part of God's dealing with us. But the stirring-up process—ah! that is hard to understand. "I cannot understand why my fortune was swept away, my companion taken, or my child called away from me." Yet the same eagle that feeds and fosters stirs up the nest and buffets the stupid fledglings. Can you see parental wisdom and kindness in the buffetings of the eagle? Then why so stupid as not to see the Father's kindness in his buffeting hand?

To me it is a grand proof of a higher destiny. If God had no better or greater destiny for us, if he did not intend that we should rise and reign in a higher realm, then he would leave us alone to sleep and dream and die in our earth nest.

"Spreadeth Abroad Her Wings."

Here we have a sublime faith picture. Faith is the lesson in Christian life. The parent eagle on the dizzy cliff height, above the awful and empty abyss, trying to induce its fledgling to leap out and off the rock into the invisible air, to risk its life upon an element that is invisible and which it has never tried—that is faith. It cannot see the atmosphere or know its sustaining power **until,** leaping into it, it finds itself upborne. Here is the soul at the point to make its first test of God's saving power. Like the invisible air, the divine power is present, though unseen and untried until the soul with a desperate faith leaps out from nature's nest to find the invisible Arms beneath it, not only upheld, but able to mount up on wings as eagles and enjoy the altitudes of a life it had never known.

"Taketh Them, Beareth Them on Her Wings."

The eye of the parent bird never turns from its young when first it tries its powers. If the atmosphere proves too heavy and the little wings begin to flag, then she takes it on her own strong wings. Here is God's present help in time of need. There is more than eagle's eye and eagle's love upon every struggling soul and more than eagle's power to sustain. How often in the conflicts of life does the atmosphere get too heavy for our strength, and it seems as if we must go down! It is then that he takes us upon the power of his wings, and we fold our wings and rest, even as the little child with folded arms at rest upon the mother's bosom. It is then that we ride on in his strength. "When I am weak, then am I strong." O the strength of life's weak hours! The sweetest season in the history of the soul is when in absolute helplessness we rest on the bosom of God.

His Protection.

There is a double purpose with the parent bird in bearing its young upon its own wings: not only to rest it, but to protect it from the shaft of the archer. When the weary wings sink down too close to the earth, there is danger. It is then that the archer's bow is bent for its destruction. But when on the parent's wing it is borne aloft and cannot be harmed unless the arrow first pierce through her own body.

How perfect the picture of God's protecting love and power! Humanity sheltered behind the cross, the death dart which had otherwise pierced us lodged in the Saviour's heart! And though he were dead, he still lives, and because he lives we shall live also. Trusting him and resting in him, we can call Omnipotence itself to our defense.

> "That soul, though all hell should endeavor to shake,
> I'll never, no never, no never forsake."

The place of safety is in the high atmosphere. We get in range of the enemy only when we get too close to the world. The ship is safest far out at sea, the eagle is safest far up in the sky, and the Christian is safest when farthest from the world.

"But," says one, "if I could reach the higher Christian life, I could not stay there." See that eagle ascending from the earth? His motion at first is heavy and labored. Slowly he toils upward; circling and re-circling, he gradually gets higher. The air gets lighter; gravitation pulls less as he gets away from the earth. He is now over the hills, beyond the mountains, above the clouds. His motion becomes easy, and his very movement is rest. Follow him now with the telescope, and there is no labor; he is but a resting speck upon the blue bosom of the upper deep.

The hard and heavy work of the Christian is to get

away from the world, to shake off the earth dews and get up and out of the heavy atmosphere. The struggling, flopping, failing, falling are all in the low atmosphere contiguous to the world. The reason we fear we could not remain in the higher experience is because we have never been there and know little of the power that sustains us.

The soul has grand possibilities in God. All his resources are pledged and at our command. It is the privilege of every soul to know that rest which is like the eagle above the storms, where gravitation is ready to turn the other way. Then let the tendency be ever upward. When the strength is spent, the wings of the Almighty are outspread to receive us. Upward, then, until nature fails and upon God's own wings we ascend to our final rest.

> "A voice within us speaks the startling word:
> 'Man, thou shalt never die!' Celestial voices
> Hymn it around our souls."

THE BROKEN BOX.

Text: "There came a woman having an alabaster box of ointment of spikenard very precious; and she brake the box, and poured it on his head." (Mark xiv. 3.)

INSIGNIFICANT things are often so linked with the heart as to stir tenderest memories. A worthless bit of faded silk—it was part of mother's dress. A battered spoon, a broken cup, a shattered toy—they bring memories of the darling one that smiled upon us and then went back to God. These old things tell of things most tender. Preachers they are that take their texts in the long ago and preach to the heart.

We come now to look at this old broken perfume box as it lies in bits before us and to gather memories it may bring or thoughts it may suggest. It was a love sacrifice, the offering of a woman, an alabaster box—a costly box made at Alabastron, in Egypt, where there was a factory for making vessels, bottles, and boxes for perfumes. This box was filled with ointment most costly and precious. It was a combination of five or six of the most costly perfumes and so valuable that Judas growled and said: "It might have been sold for more than three hundred pence." This woman came with this costly offering and, breaking the box, poured the contents upon the Master's head as he sat at meat.

Here is the offering that is well-pleasing to God. The whole East was taxed to produce it. It was a combination of all the best. We are to tax our whole being for an offering to God. One branch simply of the life and character will not suffice.

There are many "lopsided" Christians. All their spiritual thought and effort lie in one direction. All the sap flows into one branch of their religious life, while other branches are neglected and dwarfed. One is punctilious in attending church, another about meeting his obligations promptly, another about paying to the Church, while another wants to feel good all the time. Each one of these is very good, but not sufficient. The acceptable life is not one of these alone: but, like the spikenard ointment, it is all the graces, all the best things combined. We must cultivate the whole nature and then bring the best products of all as an offering to God.

This box was clean. It was pure white and spotlessly clean. Otherwise the excellence of the offering would have diminished. A lack of perfect cleanliness and purity will discount the richest feast. How often the most inviting viands are made repulsive by the manner of serving! So we have need of a clean heart in which to bring our offerings to God. Think of bearing an offering to a king in defiled and unclean hands! Think of coming to the King of kings with an offering in a heart all foul with sin! Is not this the reason that our prayers are often unanswered? Our offerings, like that of Cain, are rejected because of uncleanness of heart.

Have we spiritual deadness? Is it not because of some stain on the box, some sin spot on the unwashed heart?

> "Wash me and make me thus thine own;
> Wash me, and mine thou art;
> Wash me, but not my feet alone,
> My hands, my head, my heart."

This offering was complete. There was no reserve, but a beautiful completeness, an absolute surrender. She broke the box and poured out its precious contents. What reserves some would have made! They would have used but little of the costly unguent, just enough to perfume the head of the Master. Certainly they would not have broken the box, inasmuch as they could have had it refilled or used it for other purposes. But this woman comes with a prodigal generosity, a royal abandon, and thinks only of honoring her Lord. Hence she breaks the box, so she can never use it for any other purpose, and pours out the ointment until no drop remains. When she has finished, she has neither box nor ointment; but she has honored her Lord.

Here is a soul giving itself to God. Here is a holy recklessness, that impulse which knows no reserve. Not the giving of a fraction and keeping back the most and best to pour out upon some idol closer to the heart than Christ; no keeping of the box for other uses; no permitting of the heart to fill itself again and at any time with things of the earth; but so consecrated that it shall lie, like the broken box, at the Master's feet, a picture of worthlessness in itself, but a perpetual acknowledgment of him to whom it is given.

> "O to be nothing, nothing,
>   Only to lie at his feet,
> A broken and emptied vessel
>   For the Master's use made meet!"

The Two Estimates of This Offering.

The disciples said she was fanatical and even wickedly wasteful. Jesus said: "She hath wrought a good work on me. . . . She hath done what she could," all she could. They murmured, while Jesus commended.

Here we learn the folly of hoping to please the world or even the Church in all we do. The deed that won the Master's approval met the criticism of his own disciples. When we have done our best, like this woman, we may expect to be criticized. Sometimes when I have done all I could, poured out my soul in prayer, and given my best thought and effort and stood before God with nothing left, I have then received only evidences of dissatisfaction.

They objected to the waste. They did not object to the anointing, but would have done it with more economy. They thought they could honor the Lord and save the ointment also. This woman had missed a speculation. She had wasted what might have been sold for quite a sum. She might have made fair weather with the Master and made the gain also.

This spirit is helping to blight the Church to-day. One has a wealth of worldly pleasures; but he or she comes into the Church—ballroom, card table, theater, "nigger" minstrel and all. Another is in some sort of questionable business, but it has a fund of precious ointment in it which must not be wasted. Another wants a fat office that pays well, and he cannot let it pass simply because he has to come down from his Christian integrity and do a few questionable things. He cannot afford to let the official ointment run to waste, even if he does have to work in the dirt a little to prevent it.

Thus there are many in the Church to-day who, in place of lying as broken boxes at the Master's feet, are more like well-filled bottles marked like delicate glass, "Right side up with care." They have been made to believe that a broken and contrite spirit and a sound conversion are not necessary; that nothing is needed more than to take the vows and come into the Church. And in they come by numbers and are in no better condition than before. Like full bottles on the shelves, they sit in the pews full of self, full of the world, full of the greed of gain, and full of pride.

Yet we wonder that the Church has not more power and the word of God more effect. It is not more members, but more consecration, that is needed; not to get more people into the Church, but to get something out of those in the Church; not more fat bottles, but more broken and emptied boxes.

Jesus had only a small company, twelve in number, and they were of little worth until he got the ambition and worldliness out of them. They did, as we do now, "dispute among themselves as to who should be greatest in the kingdom." After the Master got these things out of them, they quit quarreling and were ready to die for the Master and his cause. If we but had the "broken hearts" and "poured-out lives," then would we see our Zion move with a tread that would shake the powers of darkness and the unsaved coming "as a cloud, as doves to their windows."

This offering had far-reaching effect. "She is come aforehand to anoint my body to the burying." Here is the vast reach of a perfect offering. She had no thought of his burial, but Jesus gave to her offering a dignity and meaning she did not anticipate. How our small deeds spring into significance when Christ touches them! Never did loaves and small fishes multiply as do our small services under his hand. But, like this woman, we must do what we can and all we can before he will give the uplifting touch. The little boy struck the true secret when he said to his anxious widowed mother, when the last supply of food was almost gone: "God will hear us when we scrape the bottom of the meal barrel." The prophet found another poor widow with only meal enough for one cake, but he had her bake and give that to him before he gave the perpetual supply. Yet another widow struck the Master's hand when she gave the two mites. It was all her living. So the woman of the text got his commendation only when she "brake the box" and poured out all its costly contents.

The reserves destroy the offering. There is many a wretched marriage because of a reserve in one or the other party. Christ requires our whole nature and being, "our bodies with the souls they contain, which is our reasonable service." Any reserve will destroy our joy. This woman did not clog her sacrifice with a reserve; hence it lived on and perfumed his grave and has lived and will live on until time is no more.

The balloon cannot rise until its cords are cut; neither can our offerings rise to God until we have cut the last reserve cord. The rising lark reaches the higher altitudes before you hear its notes. The soul must get loose and soar before it can sing.

This offering had an undying influence. "Wheresoever this gospel shall be preached throughout the whole world, this also that she hath done shall be spoken of for a memorial of her." The perfect offering is imperishable. It survives its author; it survives the ages. It was wrought for Christ, and hence it is deathless. Our investments for self, for gain, for pleasure, or even for comfort, will all perish; but what we do for God in the spirit of sacrifice will live forever.

It is multiplying power. This anointing was in a private home, but it went out from that home to reach the world and the ages. Nothing is so prolific as love.

When love has sown all it has, God becomes responsible for the increase. He will not allow the seed to rot or the harvest to fail. We sometimes sow for a grand harvest when we think not.

In my boyhood my father moved to the West. On the farm that he purchased was a field left idle for that year. The weeds had grown very tall, covering the field. On an autumn day I and my comrades were working our way through this weedy wilderness when suddenly we came upon the old straw pile left from the last year's threshing. There the season before the reapers had eaten melons and let the seeds fall upon the straw. Some seeds had reached the earth and had grown in greatest luxuriance, and there before us lay a wagonload of the finest melons ripening in the September sun, hidden away by the weeds, but reaching perfection.

Thus with deeds of sacrifice and kindness; they are as seeds dropped in the straw and hidden by the weeds. We cannot see them and perhaps are unaware of their existence, but they will take root and in the final autumn will come to view multiplied and beautiful.

Christ's offering has this multiplying power. There was no reserve when he laid down his life. When he said, "It is finished," he had given all. His heart, like the alabaster box, was broken. His soul, like precious ointment, was poured out. And as the ointment odor "filled all the room," the efficiency of his offering is filling the world. The seeds of his suffering are taking root everywhere. The "little stone cut from the mountain without hands" is rolling and enlarging and filling the earth. The gospel kingdom is conquering all other kingdoms. The gospel has in it that element of sacrifice which gives it claim upon every square inch of the universe. Hence opposition is powerless. "The gates of hell shall not prevail against it." It will fill the earth. It will save all that can be saved and destroy all it cannot save. "Every knee shall bow." This gospel flood is rising; but there is room for all in the air and destruction for such as refuse to fly to Christ for shelter, for "its waters shall cover the earth."

The world's redemption is the outgrowth of a perfect love sacrifice, and what we do for humanity must be done on the same principle. Are you ready to bring your heart, as the box of precious ointment, and lay it, broken and empty, at the Master's feet?

The First Language.

Text: "The heavens declare the glory of God." (Ps. xix. 1.)

THE language of the skies was the first and most simple speech, sublime as the divine and simple as childhood. This is the first language learned by the little child. It asks about the heavens and the great God that made them. It takes its first lessons from the heavenly alphabet. It asks about the great sun and the beautiful moon, as if they were the capitals, and then about the stars, which are the lesser A B C's of the heavens. We learned something of this sky language before we learned our letters. We learned it because it was simple and pleasant.

You can teach a little child more in an hour with a

map spread before it than in a day or a week without the map. God mapped the lesson on the velvet of the skies, so nicely adjusted to the sensibility of the eye. Its color never cloys. Study the heavens for an age, and they never become commonplace. Other things lose their charm. The toy pictures over which we clapped our hands with glee have long since lost their interest, but the skies are as lovely to us now as when we first asked about them in childhood. Like the old, old story, the heavens are ever new.

Not a Dead Language.

We love the speech that thrills; that eloquence which comes from an ardent soul, thrilling through the words. There is life in the language of the skies. The sun warms his words into our blood and makes us feel what he says. The stars cause us to feel the faraway touch of that providence of which they silently speak. The balmy sky subdues the soul into a sense of its own sweet serenity.

Thus we are made to feel the great divine soul back of all these speaking through them and thrilling our whole being.

A Perpetual Language.

"Day unto day uttereth speech, and night unto night showeth knowledge." There is no cessation. The succession of day and night is an unbroken and continuous proclamation of the glory of God.

These appointments are not on the itinerant plan. No annual or quadrennial change, but they stand forever. The untiring old circuit riders of the heavens continue their rounds, while the stationed preachers of the skies stand in their lot, and the work goes on from the central city of the sun even unto the outpost of the universe.

We like the fearless fidelity of these heavenly heralds. They cater to nothing, but preach, not what we wish to hear, but what God directs, whether the sermon descend in the sunbeams, distill in the dew, thunder in the tempest, burn in the drought, or sweep in the flood. We may wish the burning summer gone or the dreary winter ended, but they pursue their course, doing their work to the glory of God. Is their fidelity due to their position, far above the world and close to God? Then may we not by stubborn faith rise to a like relation and proximity to him and become fearless in every duty?

Pastoral Care.

Those ministers of the skies are not only faithful in preaching, declaring the glory of God, but they exercise a personal pastoral care over us. There is not a day in your history in which Heaven has failed to send the light at early morning to your window and to flash it along your pathway until nightfall. Whether that light was used or abused, it has come every morning to minister at your feet. No weary evening has come in which Heaven has not been prompt to shut the blinds and draw the curtains and shut out the light and make the world keep still and quiet while you slept. What is nightfall, with fading light and hushing noise? What means this general sinking of all things into silence? It is but God through nature quieting all things, that his tired children may rest and sleep. "Day unto day uttereth speech." Day by day we have this pastoral care. Do we hear that speech? Have we ears to hear what the heavens are daily speaking? There is gospel enough in a single passing day or gathering nightfall to lead the soul to God.

A Universal Language.

There is no speech or language where their voice is not heard; not a mere dialect spoken by a single community, but a language familiar to every nation under the sun. Their line, or sound, has gone out through all the earth. It is God's grand telephonic system, bringing him into communion with all nations.

However obscure or degraded the intelligence, when it takes its place beneath the skies it comes into correspondence with God. Every dewdrop, sunbeam, or shadow is an utterance declaring the grace and glory of God. That God has placed himself in communion with this world at every point and with every creature is a fact of stupendous meaning. It gives vast consequence to life. We are now in a state which pulsates with the life of God. Those must be creatures of a mighty destiny who live and move and have their being in him. It makes your home mean more since God is in it. Life means more to us since God has stooped down and is taking part in it—grand with the sight of his glory and vocal with the tones of his love.

Types the Gospel.

Rather it is the first gospel already proclaimed to every creature. But with all its glory it does not meet

God's ultimate design. It fails to reach man's moral condition and to meet his deepest want. It is too far away and too cold. It is the divine mind speaking to the human mind. It declares his glory grandly, continuously, but does not show us the divine heart. There must needs be another gospel, a speech of God's heart to our hearts. Hence God went down to the depths of his own affectional nature and brought his only and well-beloved Son and sent him to us as the expression of his love. He incorporated the language. The Word became flesh. He gave it a body with heart and blood and human nature invested with all the fullness of the Godhead, and in this form and nature he came and dwelt among us. Now we realize that he is not far off; not behind the skies and beyond the stars, but "Immanuel," God with us, and touched with the feeling of our infirmities.

How different the two gospels! The one a picture, the other a personality; one painted upon the skies, the other living in our hearts and lives. One is the beautiful yet lifeless portrait on the wall, the other the living loved one with heart and voice responsive to my own; the one is the shadow, the other the substance of love.

Easily Understood.

Like the language of the skies, it is adjusted to the child nature; the one mapped out before the mind, the other breathed into the heart by the Holy Ghost. The child old enough to know the one can also know the other. If it can know the natural sun, it can know the Sun of Righteousness, for out of the mouth of babes doth he perfect his praise. Its simplicity is its glory. The man with mind enough to commit sin has mind enough to accept Christ. The gospel at Pentecost was heard by every man in his own tongue. It is heard now by every man according to his own mental power, whether that be mighty or feeble. I am not compelled to know all the mysteries of astronomy before I can see the sun and enjoy the blessings of the heavens. I have but to lift my eyes, turn my face away from the ground, and the everlasting panorama breaks upon my vision. So I am not forced to know all the mysteries of theology in order to know Christ. I have but to lift up mine eyes and turn my face away from the world, and his pardoning love falls upon my spirit as the sunshine upon the uplifted face.

It Is to Be Universal.

When God spread the skies, he measured the reach of the gospel. We are to spread the gospel as far as the heavens declare his glory. Then let the Church look up to the visible heavens and take her reckonings; throw out her lines until they have gone through all the earth; push the gospel until its saving message has reached every creature and its words are heard to the end of the world.

We are colaborers with the sun, but ours is the more honorable ministry. The sun has warmed the world, purified its atmosphere, kissed away its dewy tears, painted its flowers, ripened its fruits, and matured its golden harvests; but it has never had the joy of carrying comfort into the home of poverty and kneeling at the bedside of dying widowhood or orphanage and whispering the story of Jesus and his love.

His light is only for a season, and it will fade; but the light that we carry to souls in sorrow will burn on when the sun is forgotten.

Brethren, be as the stars in the firmament. Though one star is different from another star in glory, yet all alike are shooting their light into the depths beneath and mingling their beams to light the world in the nighttime. "Let your light so shine before men"—let all shine forth, both great and small, until the light of the gospel shall have gone out through all the earth and its words to the end of the world, until the Master shall say, "It is enough," and call the laborers, who shall return with shouting and with everlasting joy upon their heads, bringing an evangelized world to the feet of the Son of God.

Cæsar's Penny.

Text: "Show me the tribute money. And they brought unto him a penny. And he saith unto them, Whose is this image and superscription? They say unto him, Cæsar's. Then saith he unto them, Render therefore under Cæsar the things which are Cæsar's; and unto God the things that are God's." (Matt. xxii. 19-21.)

1. This penny had passed through a process. The earth does not yield coin ready purified, molded, and stamped. No coin ever goes into circulation in the natural state in which it is taken from the earth. Its original state is one of crudeness and depravity. It must needs pass the process of pounding, washing, smelting, molding, and stamping.

Men are not born Christians any more than dimes and dollars are born of the earth. The soul in its natural state, like the coin, must pass a process of repentance and regeneration. It must be remade, made a new creature, and the divine image enstamped upon it. Whenever nature makes a coin, then we may expect her to make a Christian. When nature has produced so much as a penny molded and stamped without the ordinary process, then we may begin to believe the new doctrine of natural-born Christians. Except the dime be molded and stamped, it cannot enter the currency kingdom. Except a man be born again, he cannot see the kingdom of God.

2. Receiving the stamp identified it with Cæsar. The stamp made it relational to the head and controlling power of the empire. Insignificant within itself, yet it became at once a representative of Cæsar. More than this, it became relational to all parts of his empire and commanded an influence anywhere in his realm. It stood good for so much of any commodity handled in his realm, and it had Cæsar's honor in its keeping. While it wore his image and superscription, to discount it was to discount Cæsar and his government. It showed forth Cæsar's image to every eye that fell on it. To look on that penny was to look on Cæsar. It was Cæsar's voice in silver tones in all parts of the world.

The stamp of the new birth makes the soul relational to God, the Emperor of the universe. Insignificant we may be, but when born of God we become his representatives. More than this, we come into relation with every part and power in the moral universe and command an influence everywhere in God's kingdom. We have his honor in our keeping. While we

Autobiography of Bishop Henry Clay Morrison.

wear his image an insult to us is an insult to him, and to bring reproach upon ourselves is to bring reproach upon him and disgrace upon his government.

Like the image upon the Roman penny, the divine image should be so clear and distinct upon our life and character that no one would mistake or misjudge us. The image is sometimes so dim and indistinct that the world doubts as to where or to whom we belong. Every Christian should be a voice for God in the marts of this world.

3. The Roman Empire was responsible for that penny. It was a small affair, but to fail to redeem that penny was to compromise the honor of the empire. That penny rested its claims to regard upon the wealth of Cæsar's empire. A modest little thing, it did not undertake any great or huge enterprise. It was content to operate in a small and quiet way, but rested back in full assurance upon the wealth of the Roman government.

Thus while conversion puts us under new responsibilities to God—I say it reverently—it puts him under new responsibilities to us. As soon as we take his image his whole government becomes responsible for us. I am rather a small affair, but I have immense security behind me. God has underwritten for men: "I will never leave thee, nor forsake thee. Lo! I am with you alway." I may be the least of all, unable to work great reforms or make a stir in the Church; but, like the government which is as much responsible for the penny as for the shekel, God is as verily bound to sustain me as he was to sustain Paul, Luther, and Wesley.

4. It entered the current of commerce. This gave it influence and made it a factor in the trade of the country. It might have lain up in some miser's money box for fifty years and remained worthless. But in circulation the Roman penny could serve rich and poor, have a part in the progress of the land, and come into the presence of Christ and have direction from him.

It is the soul in circulation, the man at work in the vineyard, that gives out an influence and becomes a factor in the commerce of the moral world. The man who shrinks from every Christian duty, does nothing in the great work of saving the race, is still an immortal soul. He has a value; but, like the penny in the miser's box, he is a soul to himself and worthless to the souls of his fellow men.

The man who is not at work for Christ is not the man who will come often in contact with Christ. It was the circulation of this penny that brought it to the Master's notice. It was among the reapers that Boaz walked, and with them he conversed and not with the idlers in the shade. Christ walks among his workmen, and we feel his presence and hear his voice most frequently when we are performing his work. He superintends his work and makes himself known to his workmen.

5. Its purity had doubtless been tested. This is a suspicious world. That which wears the image of God himself is not accepted without testing. Cæsar's image did not save this penny from the testings. Men have many ways of testing coin. They weigh them, throw them violently on the counter, put *aqua fortis*

on them, and all to see if they have the right ring or will change color under the severe acids. The pure coin is proof against all these tests and comes out only the brighter.

The world has more ways to test a Christian than to test a coin. It will weigh you a hundred times over, and, like the coin thrown on the counter, it will make you feel the violence until it gets the ring of your metal. It will find what stuff you are made of. The ashes, the acids, and the *aqua fortis* will be copiously applied. The world has instruments for testing gas, oil, and whisky; but it has a thousand inventions for testing a man's religion. Yet, like the pure coin, we may have a sublime indifference to all these things, while the testing processes only bring out the brightness and purity of the character.

It is constant use that keeps the coin bright. Our religion increases in beauty by its activity. The most beautiful characters in the Church are those who under affliction, unable to be active, are quite submissive and sweet-spirited sufferers. No penny can be made bright without use.

6. In my fancy I heard an old-time ten-cent piece telling its experience. It was old and well worn, but had withal a very bright face. It said: "I am a very small coin and never made a great stir in the world, but I have been stirring all my life. I cannot tell all my experience, only a small part of it, and you must judge the balance. When I came from the mint, there were about ten thousand of us bright-faced comrades; but we soon got separated, and what became of my companions I have never known. I had no time to

look after them, for I have been kept moving. I went into the hands of a merchant and was given out in change. I helped to pay a man's tax, and then I paid for a cigar—a thing I did not wish to do—and then, worse than all, I was given in exchange for a drink of whisky. I was greatly mortified at this. I then went into a street car money box and paid the fare of a tired old man. I afterwards went to church and was picked out from a lot of larger coins and put into the contribution box. I then helped to buy a pair of shoes for the parsonage baby, and then I got out again into the wide world, and thus I have been going on for forty years. I was never worth more than ten cents, but by dint of energy and never stopping I have paid hundreds of dollars. I have served rich and poor and benefited them just as far as they have used me rightly. I am a very unworthy dime, but have done what I could."

Here is a Christian experience. We separate very soon from those with whom we begin the life battle. We go into all the affairs of the political, social, domestic, and civil economy of life. We do some good things and make some mistakes; but if we have pure motives and keep moving, we will in the course of a lifetime be made a blessing to multitudes, even though we are never worth more than a dime. And it is a fact that the lesser coins are most in circulation. This coin that settled the great question put to the Master was only a penny. The larger coins are too big to get about much. They do not go through the hands of the paper boy and the rag picker and the peasant and the homeless widow. It is the little ones that have the most opportunities for doing good. Let the smaller coin cease from circulation, and commerce is well-nigh crushed; let the little ones cease their efforts for God, and his cause is well-nigh hopeless.

7. The image and superscription gave the penny its direction. It was the image upon it that sent it to Cæsar. This will be repeated in the final day. When the battle is over and the life work done and we stand with a congregated world at the judgment of God, the question then will be, "Whose image is upon him?" Then let us be sure we have that image now. Bury the dime and leave it in the earth until that last day, and the image will still be upon it. Earth and time cannot destroy that image. If we have God's image now, the ages that may pass before that last day of reckoning will not efface it. It will then be said again, "Render unto God the things that are God's," and we will go from that judgment to be with him forever.

The Donation Party.

Text: "And the men took that present, . . . and rose up, and went down to Egypt, and stood before Joseph." (Gen. xliii. 15.)

CANAAN was in famine. God needs famines in the government of the world as much as he needs gravitation or sunshine. In a severe drought we heard an infidel remark: "How greatly we are suffering for rain!" We replied: "Some men can get along very well without a God except in a drought or an epidemic. It is very awkward in time of distress to have no one to whom to go for help."

But for this famine, Jacob would never have found

his long-lost son, and Egypt would never have known the true God. Calamity can outstretch good fortune in moral effect. Calamity will tear up and subsoil the nature, and it is the deep plowing that brings richest growth.

Their Condition.

This was beyond description—rain withheld, vegetation dead, animals perishing, earth baked, heavens brassy, and atmosphere thick with stifling dust.

Famine pictures humanity out of Christ. The famine has been sore in man's moral nature since the fall. The sin that dried Eden's fountains dried the wellsprings in man's moral being. Since the divine life was cut off, humanity has been morally destitute. Its best powers, like the animals in famine, are paralyzed, weak, and staggering; its moral beauty gone, as the glow of health from the face of famine. The little supply which the soul can gather from the world is, like Jacob's supply of corn, soon exhausted. How rapidly the supply goes when the article is very scarce! The soul soon consumes the little corn it can glean from this world. Pleasures cloy, age advances, tastes grow dull, the senses fail, and the keen relish for the world is gone; while the soul in wrinkled age asks, as did Jacob, where it may buy a little food.

How pitiable the picture of old age trying to rekindle its dying embers and coax back the flying phantoms of an abused and misspent youth! Thousands, young and old, are thus employed to-day; the one exhausted by age, the other by dissipation. One offered a reward to any one who would invent a new pleasure, and the wrecks of humanity offer all they have for a little more of the joys of earth.

The Terms Offered Them.

They could return to Egypt on one condition. That was that they bring Benjamin. Joseph had said: "Ye shall not see my face, except your brother be with you." Joseph loved his father and his unfortunate brothers. He knew their desperate condition. He had the desire that a great nature has to return good for evil; yet they must trust him implicitly. Jacob is his father, but even he cannot have supplies until he has trusted his darling Benjamin into the power of a man of whom he knows nothing.

Who cannot see in this pathetic case the type of a higher transaction? Here is the one and only condition on which God accepts the penitent sinner. This is a day of soft gospel. We hear much of how God loves us, and so he does. Joseph loved his father and his brothers, but he required Benjamin. God loves the sinner, but will never receive and save him until he gives up his idols and trusts him with an implicit trust.

Necessity Often the Basis of Trust.

Naked necessity has driven many a soul to Christ who never would have trusted him otherwise. Gaunt, grim, red-handed necessity is often sent of God as the shepherd sends his well-trained dog to bring the straying sheep to alarm and, if need be, to bite the erring soul and drive it back to Christ.

It was starvation that made Jacob trust and let Benjamin go. If the bread corn had only held out,

Benjamin would never have seen Egypt. The story of the prodigal son hasn't so much poetry, after all. It was a case of starvation. He would never have gone back home had he not struck bottom. His repentance began in the gnawing of an empty stomach. Better begin there than not at all. No matter how repentance begins, so it goes through and through and brings the sinner to Christ.

Æsthetics and high notions may be well enough when a man gets financially to the top, but they are a great hindrance when he has to begin on nothing. Let a young man begin life with nothing but high notions, a sort of cambric-and-kid-glove apprentice, and he will never do much. So in the matter of repentance. Some people are very æsthetic and tony in their ideas of repenting. They say: "I am going to repent from principle and not from fear. I could not have the face to call upon God when about to die after having ignored him all my life when in health." Well, I would have just that much face. If I had never prayed, I would pray then. Those who repent on the kid-glove-and-cambric principle are about as successful in their repentance as a dude would be as a hod-carrier.

When a man is in need he will take work, if he can get it, without the æsthetics. And when a man wants to be saved he doesn't stand on the niceties of his repentance. No matter how he has lived or what he has done, he will pray to God for mercy and pardon. His very desperation will give him courage.

Jacob's great need did not kill his joy when he was relieved. His gladness in Joseph and the plenty of

Egypt were none the less because hunger drove him there. The disappointments and dead-sea fruit of this world will even make our relish the keener for heavenly joys. The Goshen milk and butter tasted sweeter to Jacob and his sons because of his having been half starved. Think of a man in heaven moping around and in a pout because he had repented on high principles! No, no! That we are allowed to repent at all is a miracle of grace.

The Preparation to Start to Egypt.

Jacob said, "If it must be so now, do this; . . . carry down the man a present, a little balm, and a little honey"—and it was a little and more wax than honey—"spices and myrrh, nuts and almonds: and take double money"—he had more money than corn—last of all, "take also your brother, and arise, go again unto the man."

It was an immense tax, in their famished condition, to get up a benefit for Joseph. Joseph had not demanded any of their pitiable products. He demanded but one thing: that they bring Benjamin.

See the picture. Here they are, lean and hungry, not having had a full meal for weeks, but struggling to keep up appearances. Haven't you seen proud poor people trying to keep up and do just as rich people do? We have here our party with their petty sacks, buckets, baskets, budgets, and bundles, with a little of the sorriest fruit and nuts and honey that the world ever saw. With all this, and mounted on their little skinny, staggering donkeys, they set out to carry a present to the chief officer of the richest empire on earth! If there ever was a perfect picture of the "shabby genteel," here it is. Perhaps here is where Dickens got his idea.

They took the present and the money and Benjamin and went down and stood before Joseph. I fancy the very servants snickered and required effort to suppress laughter. "Poor white trash" trying to keep up appearances and make their master believe they were somebody!

But for Joseph's love and sympathy the whole thing would have been contemptible and an offense to his royal personage and position.

Here Is Human Nature.

It doesn't like to come to God at all and waits until compelled, then brings its miserable products, trying to keep up appearances. Canaan in famine never had sorrier fruits than the unregenerate soul has in its native depravity. A man trying to get good enough to come to Christ is like Jacob's sons trying to pick out a decent present for Joseph. He gathers up a little common honesty, a little morality, with a dried bunch or two of good intentions—the whole of it like the Canaanitish honey that wouldn't squeeze out two ounces of honey to a pound of wax—not an ounce of moral essence in the whole thing, and yet with this miserable offering he comes before God, expecting to find favor. It is worse than the ten lank Hebrews at the door of Joseph's palace.

Note Their Reception.

After all their plans and picking and culling and care, Joseph takes no notice whatever of their donation. It is not even mentioned. But when he saw Benjamin he said to the ruler of his house: "Bring these men home, for they shall dine with me at noon." Benjamin, the old father's idol, was all he wished to see. Benjamin is here, and Joseph's only demand is met. The patriarch has surrendered and given his idol up to a strange prince.

Here is what God demands: not the fruits of famished human nature; not what we can put out and parade before him; but he demands a Benjamin, the idol, that pet lust or pleasure or indulgence that lies back in the soul's bosom which we love better than we love God. God calls for that. We cannot see his face except this be given up. It is part with Benjamin or perish. Give up your soul's idol or perish eternally.

Their Kinship Saved Them.

It was well they had a brother who was full brother to Joseph. Men make a jest of being brother-in-law and half brother to the Church. Joseph had ten half brothers to one full brother. Jesus, like Joseph, always had more distant kin than any other kind. The half brothers had perished but for their kinship to the full brother. They were just enough kin to Joseph to make them feel mean. They felt worse when they found out who Joseph was than if they had been of no kin at all. This half brothership to Christ is a poor affair. Some people have just enough religion to make them uncomfortable. I pray you to-day, let us seek a closer kinship to the Master.

Our Elder Brother is the Son of God, and our kinship to him is our salvation. Like Joseph's brethren, we have sinned and sold our Elder Brother for less than the traders paid them for Joseph; yet, after all, we are saved through our kinship to Christ. Coming to God, we have but to bring Christ, as the ten brought Benjamin, and we shall have access and find peace with God.

With what joy did Joseph take that noonday meal with his brethren, giving his bounties into the very hands which in his ladhood had cast him into the pit, feeding the very ones who had sold him to the traders and dipped his coat in blood and showed it to his father that he might mourn him as dead! Now he saves them from starvation and honors them at his royal table.

There is a reception in waiting for the penitent soul more royal than that of Jacob's sons. At the marriage supper of the Lamb, Christ himself shall serve us. The hands through which we drove the nails and which dripped with blood for us—from those hands shall we receive heavenly ministries and the crown of life.

WITHHOLDING THE HEART.

Text: "Thou gavest me no kiss." (Luke vii. 45.)

CHRIST was dining with a Pharisee, a man of morals and strait-laced in his religion. He doubtless entertained with dignity, and his hospitality was all it should have been save a lack of heart in it—like some elaborate occasions you have seen, where everything was very fine and full on the outside, while you felt the conventionality beneath the profuse surface.

Simon, the host, is a representative man. He represents the radical and fatal defects which may exist in a blameless life. He is both a moralist and a religionist. His religion is a factor in his life. His fasts, his prayers, his almsgiving are notable. He is careful of contaminations and is surprised that the Master permits the Gentile woman to touch him. The Master utters no criticism, but suggests the lack of heart in his hospitality. "Thou gavest me no kiss."

There may be great beauty combined with radical defects. Indeed, beauty is often the covering that conceals corruption. Fruit decayed at the core has the most delicate blush on the surface. The bewitching foxglove hides its poison beneath its beauty. The hectic flush mistaken for health is but the deceptive covering of death.

As in nature, so in grace: there may be the signs of soundness where all is decay. A man may be moral, churchly, punctilious in duty, and yet be a hypocrite. Simon had not failed on morals or Churchism, neither in courtesy to the Master; but he had given him no kiss of love. His heart was not involved in his hospitality.

Note the meaning of a kiss. The mind can always express itself in words, but the heart often carries burdens too weighty for language. When a matter gets deep enough to involve the heart, language is apt to fail. You hear one say: "I have no words to express my gratitude for this kindness." That means it has reached the deep waters of the heart. Hence when the heart cannot put itself into words it resorts to kisses, embraces, tears, laughter, shouting.

"Simon, since I came into thy house thou hast given

me no kiss. Thy heart has not so much as uttered a syllable of love; while this woman hath washed my feet with her tears, bathed them in the liquid love of her grateful heart, and, taking that which is her glory and bending down in humility, hath wiped them with the hairs of her head. Thou gavest me no kiss; but she hath not ceased to kiss my feet. Thou hast spoken to me only in words that die on the air, while she hath uttered no word; but her heart has spoken in kisses and in tears."

Love evidences the new life. We know that we have passed from death unto life, not because we have stood at the chancel and publicly "denounced the devil and all his works, the vain pomp and glory of the world," but because we love God and love the brethren, because we love to linger at the feet of the Master, pouring out our hearts in gratitude and giving to him our best offerings.

Satan would, if he could, take all heart out of the Church, and he comes dangerously near it sometimes when he gets people to think it is a weakness to shed tears and almost a disgrace to allow the heart to express its impulses. No wonder the Church gets cold and formal. If the Saviour's feet were never washed until you got tears enough out of some of the worldly and fashionable Churches of the present time, they would go unwashed, as they did at Simon's dinner.

How is it with our hearts to-day? I dare say Simon had a plethoric pocketbook, set a good table, had a pew in the synagogue, and attended services every Sunday; but his soul was dried up. He did not feel like kissing the Master, and he had no tears to shed.

Kissing is a dry business where there is no love, and weeping is hard work when the heart is dried up.

The winds of worldliness dry the soul, as the east wind dried the sea bed before marching Israel—winds that blow through theaters and around euchre tables, stirring excitement, blowing up prizes, and dashing world dust into Methodist eyes; winds from questionable enterprises and occupations that dazzle and blind the eyes of the soul, darkening the spiritual vision with the dust of gold. These things dry the love fountains and leave no impulse to pour out the soul in worship and to kiss the feet of Him who loved us and gave Himself for us and whose body and blood are emblems before us this morning.

Love is the chief power. God made us to love him and has given us capacity to love him in a multitude of forms. The heart is God's kingdom, and some one has said: "The heart is capable of as great a variety of loves as the vineyard is of wines." In the vineyard you will see every variety of grape gathered and cultivated by the skillful vinedresser—the dark, the purple, the white, and the deep, rich red; grapes of every color, size, and excellence—yet each has a sweetness and flavor peculiar to itself, all excellent, yet all different.

Thus with the blood-washed heart; it is God's vineyard. He made it for the varieties of loves—the filial, the parental, the conjugal, and the national—all loves from the same heart, all sweet and noble, but different. We may love God with a variety of loves. We love his omnipotence, and before it the soul lies prostrate and in silent awe. We love his omniscience and rejoice in the consciousness of his constant presence with us. We love his forbearance and worship that divine patience which has borne with us and never grown tired. But above all we love the deep, rich, red grace of redemption as it wells up from the heart of God, presses its way adown the ages, descends in human form, and, being lifted up, pours itself in a crimson tide upon humanity; that love which lies in the simple emblems now before us and of which we are now to partake. It is this that calls forth our best worship.

Love is God's only demand. After all his investments for us he exacts but one thing in return: that is our love. "Thou shalt love the Lord thy God with all thy heart." Love is the only commodity taken in exchange for his mercies. You pay your money into the Church, but no penny of it goes up to God. What you pay and what you do may come back upon yourself and others as the sea water falling back again in the spring rain. But he calls for our love, as if it were a necessity to his divine and perfect nature and as if he could not be satisfied without it. He has been somehow with men from the beginning, trying to get their love. He came into our world and in our form and into our sufferings and lived and taught and suffered and died among us that he might win our love. Have we denied him this one and only costless thing that he asks? Can he say of us, as he said to Simon, "Thou hast given me no kiss"? Are we here to-day, Simon-like, morally prim, decently pious, wrapped in a respectable Churchism, and feeling glad that we are not as other men—a people altogether worthy of ourselves—while keeping back the heart's true worship and the kiss of love from the Master?

We come to this sacrament, not to meet his wisdom or his power, but his love. This sacrament is the speech of his heart, a heart broken of love for us. Shall we come with no response? As we touch and taste these emblems shall we not by simple faith give to our risen and ascended Lord the heart's true kiss of love?

THE TIMELY COMING.

Text: "Come before winter." (2 Tim. iv. 21.)

1. IT was Timothy's only chance to see Paul. Timothy was at Ephesus; Paul was in prison at Rome. Paul loved him as his own life and above all others preferred to have him with him in his last imprisonment and final martyrdom. But great as was his love and intense as was his anxiety to see Timothy, he could take no step toward Ephesus, where Timothy lived. His prison walls confine him. His thought and heart go out to Timothy; but if they should ever meet, Timothy must come to him. He is at liberty, while Paul is bound. The greater must wait upon the less. He cannot go to him, but from within his prison he sends the message to hasten Timothy's coming: "Come before winter."

Here is illustrated the relation of the sinner and the Saviour. The sinner must come to Christ if the two ever meet. The greater is bound, while the lesser is free. Christ has made all the advance that he can make. He has approached the sinner on every side and loved him even unto death. He has done all and reached the point where he can do no more. His own eternal principles and the sinner's sovereign will prevent him from nearer approach. They hold him from the sinner as the prison walls held Paul from Timothy. Sinner, despite all his love and solicitude for your salvation, he must await your coming. He sends his love to you in sweet persuasiveness to induce you to do what he cannot do for you—yield your will and come unto him. "Him that cometh unto me I will in no wise cast out." And, like Paul urging Timothy, he urges you to come before winter.

2. The winter was advancing. Each sunset left the time shorter and the possibilities less for these two to meet, who loved each other so dearly; and Paul, anticipating, foreseeing the winter, urges haste.

Such is true with each one hearing me now. The winter is advancing. It may be full summer time now—the full vigor of life, the warm flow of healthy blood, soul full of music and merriment, hair glossy, eyes sparkling, cheek flushed and no furrows from time's plowshare across the brow—but still winter is approaching. Anticipate, throw thought but a little way into the future, and the summer season is gone, and the sadness of autumn is upon the life. Like the forest, life is in the sear and yellow leaf. The swallows have gone, the sun is farther away; there is a chill in the air, a moaning in the leafless boughs. Visions of spectacles, walking canes, reclining chairs, and dying couches come in view. The dim eyes seem to see snow falling. many heads are whitening, and there come echoes of distant storms. It is winter.

These things will soon be as familiar to you as the poetic surroundings of your present and buoyant youth.

3. But what does winter mean? It means change in heaven, earth, and air. It means cutting off facilities, multiplying difficulties, and increasing the dangers of travel. It means rough and dangerous roads and tempestuous and hazardous seas. It was a journey to Rome that thickened with difficulties as winter advanced.

Your journey to the better land is like that of Timothy to Rome; its hindrances and obstacles multiply as winter approaches. Winter cuts off outward influences and represses inward forces. It withers the flowers and blasts the foliage, shuts out the sunshine and beclouds the skies; it petrifies the singing streams and makes the naked trees stand shivering in the blast. There is no poetry in winter, and all the growing forces are repressed.

How different in summer time! The forces within and the influences without are all positive. They rise and flow out. The forces are aggressive; life bursts forth everywhere. The air is balmy; bees hum, birds sing, children romp, and even the invalid in his chair is drawn to the front porch. How magnetic, how helpful these springtime influences! Can we not feel the lesson and why we should come before winter?

4. Come while the forces and influences are helpful. There is in life's springtime an outflow of the spiritual forces and a power in the outward gospel influences. As the flowers are responsive to the sunshine, so are childhood and youth responsive to holy influences.

Many times the child heart is drawn out by gospel magnetism and desires to give itself to God and join the Church and be a Christian when perhaps the unwise parent will repress it.

Sad! Sad! Better, like the Chinese, bind the child's feet or, like the Indians, put its head in a clamp and grow it flat and out of shape rather than repress the growth of the little spirit as it is unfolding toward God. There are so many things that are helpful to youth in coming to Christ. Let me exhort you to come while the tides are helpful. Come while the winds waft you that way. Come before winter. Do not wait. When the winter of old age comes, there will be a reversion. The influences which now move you toward Christ will set in the opposite direction. Your affections frozen, your impulses dead, your conscience benumbed, your spirit chilled—there will be winter within and without that will militate against your coming.

Paul wished Timothy to come before winter, knowing that if he did not he would most likely not come at all. How high is this probability in your case? If a man passes the periods of childhood and youth, resisting all the influences, how probable it is that in the winter of life, with its tides against him and inward desires dying out, he will never come to Christ at all!

5. The dangers of deathbed repentance are not a few. First, there may be no such bed for you. Thousands die with no moment of warning. The street, your office, your pew, your table—any of these may be the place of your death. Again, your mind may be

unbalanced and no power left for the great matter in which all life centers. Pain may be so intense as to forbid a moment's composure or self-command. Winter may be so completed in your soul that no feeling can be awakened, and the sense of your lifetime disregard for the things of God may help to repel and prevent your being saved at that final hour.

However, allowing that you escape all these things, what have you at such an hour to offer to God? A body worn out and consumed by sin and the service of self and the world; not strength left to do anything for God or humanity; a poor, decaying clod that cannot lift itself from its pillow or so much as wipe the death damp from its own brow; a soul undeveloped, withered, shriveled, polluted, and consumed by sin. And this is the offering, this soul, this body; these constitute the offering, the insult that you bring at last to God. Truly this is a winter's offering. Such a deathbed is a wintry place. Such a scene, such a picture is freezing to the spirit. O, my friend, come to Christ now! Come while you have something of life's summer time to bring. Come before winter.

NOTHING FOR BREAKFAST.

Text: "Then Jesus saith unto them, Children, have ye any meat? They answered him, No." (John xxi. 5.)

HERE is a company of seven disappointed and discouraged men. They had left all to follow Christ, and now he has been captured and crucified, and their fondest hopes are blighted. Now their question is, "What shall we do? We had great notions of a great kingdom and even quarreled as to who should be greatest in that kingdom. We had multitudes to follow us, and we even worked miracles; but now our Leader is dead, our power is gone, and we are hopeless. It will be almost a shame to go back to the old occupation. Had we better use our experience in miracle-working and set up a sleight-of-hand show or a lottery? The Damascus valleys are fine for grain; can't we trade in futures and recover from our bankrupt condition? What shall we do?" Peter said: "I go a-fishing."

The Power of Right Example.

Peter could have said: "I understand the fishing business better than lotteries or futures. I know that is honest and honorable, and I can net the fish of Galilee without swindling any one even in a legalized way. Furthermore, the Master called me from that business, and I am going quietly back to it and await developments. I don't know what you all intend doing, but I go a-fishing." They answered: "We shall also go with thee." Peter's decision carried the whole company. How strong is right example in an emergency when put promptly and without equivocation! What a blessing is a strong, right character in a company or community when right action is needed! When disaster has left everything in wreck, just to have some strong, true spirit lead the way to retrieve the lost fortune!

Demoralization often begins in disaster. Men aim for high things and fail; they cannot consent, like Peter, to go back and take up their old nets and don the old fisher's coat again. Something else must be devised to make money faster than by the old way. Failure is often the mother of fraud. Humbugs and cheats rise Phœnixlike from the ashes of misfortune. Few men when they have gotten away from the smell of the fishery and held prominent positions and had their loaves and fishes served to hand without labor on their part have the courage to go back and wade the waters and drag the net.

Failure Followed Failure.

They went forth immediately and fished all night and caught nothing. Everything was favorable; nighttime was the best time for catching fish; they were expert fishermen; they put forth their best efforts and toiled till daydawn and took nothing. The morning light revealed another and an utter failure. Their princely prospects were blighted, and now their old occupation was gone. The very sea, always so liberal to them, had closed its hand; and there they were in the morning twilight cold, wet, fatigued, discouraged, hungry, and without meat.

Life Without Christ.

Life without Christ is a nighttime and a scene of failure, a time of toil and weariness and nothing taken. Honest men, experienced men go into life's activities, as these men dragged the waters of Genessaret, and drag the waters of the life channel through all the years, and the whole life proves a financial water haul. Old age finds them tired and worn and poor, as when they started. Some of the few who succeed financially take nothing for the soul. Find the man who has grown rich without Christ, and you find one who has made an eternal water haul. Ask him as he stands on the shore of eternity if his soul, his eternal self, has any meat, and he will answer as the fishermen answered the Master, "No." He closes life weary, starving, and without hope. These men have toiled all night, not only without Christ, but even without faith in him. Now they stand empty-handed, while the very sea mocks them with its calm indifference.

Here is a life picture. There are thousands now who line the banks and stand along the shores of life disappointed, helpless, hopeless. And why? Simply because they have toiled without Christ. Let life be never so honest, honorable, and sincere; without Christ it is failure and only failure.

The Manifestation.

When the morning was come, Jesus stood on the shore. Notice, he presents himself just at their point of despair. He had watched them in their toil; perhaps he had ordered that they should take nothing, that they might see his power. Had they caught all the fish they wanted, then the hundred and fifty and three would have made less impression. Success often shuts us out from seeing our Lord.

It is the manner of the Master to show himself in our most pitiable conditions rather than in our greatest successes. It is at the end of our strength that we touch the divine finger tips. When you get to where you can go no farther and do nothing more, then look for the coming of the Master. He is the God of the extreme hours, the present help in time of need. You found him first just as your sins seemed sinking you to despair. I have never passed a close place or a trying juncture in life where I did not meet him.

The Question.

"Have you any meat?" He knew they had none, but he would have them feel their failure and confess their want. They confessed they had no meat. Then said he: "Cast the net on the right side of the ship, and ye shall find." They cast, therefore, and now they are not able to draw it for the multitude of fishes. Here is the difference between work in our own strength and work in the strength of God—a whole night's toil with nothing but disappointment, and now the same men with the same net and in the same place by a single cast have more than they can draw to shore. What made the difference? They gave up hope of self-success and cast as Christ directed.

The lesson is plain. Are you a disappointed fisherman in the stream of life? Have you dragged its waters till you are weary and taken nothing? No meat for your soul? Nothing that satisfies? Has all your life's labor given you nothing to feed and satisfy your immortal nature? Then what will you do? Despair? Never! Never! Christ watches you with like loving interest with which he watched the weary fishermen. Perhaps he has ordered some of your failures and is waiting for your very weariness to drive you to him. He says to you now: "Take up the net and cast it on the right side." You have toiled with the net on the wrong side. Your thought and affection have been in the wrong direction. Take up the life net and put it on the other side, the right side, the Christ side.

They did not get a new net. It was the same net they had dragged with all night. Take the same heart, the same affection you have been giving to the things of the world and give them to Christ. They did not go to hunt a better place to fish. So you need not hunt better environment, but right where you are and right now: in your home, with family cares and perplexities of everyday life; right in your place as a business man; right where you have been so long and so unhappy. There and now by Christ's direction you can make such a draft, gather such blessing and satisfaction that you cannot contain it. Cast on the right side. Tell me, you who have made the test, when you cast heart and life on the right side did you not find peace, rest, and fullness of joy more than heart could contain or tongue express? Weary soul, cast on the right side to-day.

The Recognition.

"When the morning was come, Jesus stood on the shore; but the disciples knew not that it was Jesus." And when by his direction they inclosed the great multitude of fishes, even then they supposed him only a fellow fisherman who happened to know just the best side on which to cast the net. But there was one among the number who could see more than mere good luck in that haul. Therefore that disciple whom Jesus loved said to Peter: "It is the Lord." Why does John recognize him first? He is the youngest and least experienced. Ah! his love for Christ was perhaps the most intense, the far-seeing insight of love. Nothing is so quick on recognition as love.

See in yonder cottage. It is past midnight; a dim light flickers through the lattice. A weeping mother is watching a dying child. The husband and father is away from home. She has hoped and prayed for his coming. Half a dozen friends and neighbors watch with her. The hours are wearing away, when the silence is broken by a faint footfall in the distance. Nearer and nearer it approaches. To that company it is only the tramp of a watchman or a belated stranger. But that anxious wife hears that step, listens but a moment, and her sad face brightens as she says: "Thank God, husband is coming! I know his footstep. He will see our darling once more while yet alive." Love knows even the footfall of its love.

Thus John knew Jesus. "It is the Lord." It is his way to come when we are not expecting him, when we are discouraged and in trouble. "He came that way when we were in the storm on this very lake. It was in the fourth watch, and just as we were about to give up and perish he came to us, walking upon the sea. He did the same thing when we were going to Emmaus, and our hearts were sad and full of sorrow; but he blessed us before we parted from him. That was the way he came to us in the prayer meeting when Thomas was not there." They knew it was the Lord; they could see his hand in the full and almost breaking net.

Even He Cannot Hide from Love.

When we love him we can see him in everything, in every smile of providence, in every abundant harvest, in every timely kindness of a friend. We can even see him in life's adversities. Love learns that the clouds are his chariots; hence it looks for him especially in the clouds, in misfortunes, calamities, and sad happenings.

> "Judge not the Lord by feeble sense,
> But trust him for his grace.
> Behind a frowning providence
> He hides a smiling face."

It takes the keen penetration of love to pierce the frowning providence and detect the smiling face. How beautiful that love which detects the footfall of the Master in the ways and walks of life!

The Breakfast.

"As soon as they were come to land, they saw a fire of coals there, and fish laid thereon, and bread." The breakfast was ready, fresh and warm, the fish not yet taken off the coals. It was a meal with all the fresh fervors, no warmed-over, second-hand affair.

How eternally independent of land and sea! The sea may refuse to yield up another fish and earth decline to produce another loaf, yet Christ has supplies ever ready for his needy children. His blessings, like the seaside meal, are ever fresh and warm and rich. There is nothing stale in all the bill of fare in divine grace. Every blessing seems the best because fresh from his hand.

He Honored Their Work.

He said: "Bring of the fish ye have now caught, and come and dine." Bring of your fish and let them be part of the repast. He will share with them and honor their work. Our life toil may have little success; but he will own and honor what we are able to do, be it ever so insignificant. The souls we bless and make better in this life will be to us a constant future joy. Their love will come back upon us an exceeding and eternal weight of glory. Our work, however small, will be a part of the soul feast in eternity.

The Picture.

The weary fishermen, the dawning light, the waiting Lord, the landed net, the ready feast, the happy communion—here is Christian life in its final close. In the final morning dawn Jesus will be standing on the shore waiting for us.

We are now in the life stream dragging the net. The Church is committed to our care. Every Christian is a fisher of men. The work is grand, though sometimes discouraging. The waters are cold, the winds keen, the toil heavy, and the rocks sharp and cutting to the feet. But with it all Jesus waits upon the shore, and we will get to land at last, bringing with us some whom we have won in his name, under his direction. Then shall we hear the welcome and see the ready feast, a feast as far above the seaside breakfast as heaven is above Genessaret. Then will the invitation be: "Enter into the joys of thy Lord."

"I go a-fishing." Let others do as they may, we propose to continue the toil until we see the Lord in the twilight of eternity's morning waiting for us on the shining shore. Will you join us to-day and give your life to Christ and to the work of drawing the gospel net?

Obstacles Overcome.

Text: "And he sought to see Jesus who he was; and could not for the press, because he was little of stature. And he ran before, and climbed up into a sycamore tree to see him: for he was to pass that way." (Luke xix. 3, 4.)

Hopeless cases are common things. The physician finds them, the preacher finds them, the teacher finds them, and Church and State find them; but Christ never did. Whether a dying thief, a woman with seven devils, or a man so full of devils and so fierce as to be a terror and to dwell among the tombs, none were hopeless under his hand.

Here is a man least likely to be saved, a rich city officer, a sort of bloated bondholder, as little likely to be converted as a ruling prince in a bucket shop or a whisky king with an invested million. It takes a gospel with divine power to awaken such a man and make him desire to see another man who was poorer than the foxes or the birds.

He was rich, but dissatisfied—the condition of all such men. Riches are but wretchedness until we know Christ. A man may be rich in goods, in fame, or even rich in influence, yet without Christ he is never at rest. He may have comfort, ease, luxury, and splendor; but the heart, the inner self, like the compass needle, is unsettled and tremulous until it rests in Christ.

The multitude hid Christ from his view—a multitude of people larger than himself, such as entirely prevented him from seeing the passing Nazarene. "He could not see for the press, because he was little of stature." He saw he had no chance while in the crowd; he knew that when the crowd had passed the Saviour would have passed also. Hence if he saw him at all he must extricate himself from the multitude.

Whenever a soul feels a desire to see Christ, there begins to be a press of the multitude. Pride and passion and self and love of the world and fear of criticism and carnal appetites and fleshly lusts—all that army of things which war against the soul will begin their pressure. They encompass and shut off the view—things mighty and tall and giantlike. We struggle against them, and, like him who was little of stature, we are thrown back and "cannot because of the press." The sooner we realize our inability to cope with these things, the sooner we will get to Christ. What a picture of helplessness and baffled hope is a little man in a vast, excited crowd, putting forth all his strength, now thinking for a moment that he will succeed, then in a twinkling hurled back hopelessly to where he started!

Here is one trying to see or serve Christ who has not forsaken the multitude, that multitude of things which war against the soul. The only hope is to get away from these things. Extricate yourself, part company with that crowd, no matter how many things in it which have been dear and lovable to you in the past.

Here is the why of poor religious progress. There are thousands desiring and even trying to serve God and failing because they will not leave the multitude. These people even in the press sometimes catch a glimpse of the Master and are made unspeakably happy; then some towering habit or appetite or earthly idol steps in between, and the Master is hidden from view. The only chance for a peaceful and abiding view of Christ is to part company with the multitude, these unfriendly things. Get out of this crowd and get free from the press.

How He Escaped the Crowd.

He ran before, did not wait for the multitude to get out of his way, neither for a chance opening that might give him access to Christ; but he "made haste and ran" in advance of the throng and so situated himself that he could see the Master in spite of the crowd. He overcame his own disability (littleness of stature) and mastered all the disadvantages occasioned by the press by simply running before them. Here is the secret of religious success—being in haste and running in advance of the multitude. The multitude that will keep men from coming to Christ increases daily.

The one who runs before starts in early life, gets in advance of the ever-increasing evils which are inherent in our nature and the cares and responsibilities of later life; that one is likely to get the best view and have the closest relation to the Master. There is all advantage in being ahead of the multitude.

Some are waiting for the crowd to pass. The crowd passed that day on the Jericho road, but Christ passed with the crowd. The multitude of things now keeping you from Christ will pass. Those cares and interests and idols and worldly loves and questionable habits now intervening and absorbing your thought will all pass. The day is coming when they will have gone, but Christ will have gone with them.

Autobiography of Bishop Henry Clay Morrison.

The old man who has seen life's multitudes all pass, its years and cares and experiences come and go, without knowing Christ will stand alone in the quiet hush of life's evening time, and the distant din of the receding multitude will fall faint upon his dull hearing, while his dim eyes are strained in a vain effort to see the Son of God. It is too late then; he will have passed. But he has not passed yet, and we are here to lift a voice above the roar of the thronging, pressing multitude and tell you in glad tones: "Jesus of Nazareth passeth by."

He rose above conventionalities. He climbed up into a sycamore tree to see him. For a man of position and prominence to be scrambling up a tree by the public highway was not the most dignified performance, viewed from a Chesterfieldian standpoint. But from the standpoint of a penitent, a man trying to come to Christ, acting from the deep impulses of his heart, the lack of propriety is not so marked. There is a dignity which God observes in every movement of a penitent soul. The cry for mercy, the groan over sins, the hallelujah of the newborn soul—these have a dignity and a moral majesty which are far above social conventionalities.

What are the customs and requirements by which we regulate our relations to each other in social life? What are all these things to God? Not so much as the manners of mice are to us. What of ceremony and dignity when the President of the United States is to pass through your city or town? Old and young, rich and poor, black and white are going to see him if it is possible. They will stand on boxes or barrel heads and climb to house roofs and hire front windows at any cost. Dignity and ceremony go to the winds until they see the President, who is to pass that way. Still, some of those very people who will tumble over each other trying to get to see a poor, miserable sinner in the person of a President are very decorous and squeamish about the way in which people should act who are trying to get to Christ. I should like to see just one up-to-date, latest-fad, one-thumb-out-of-his-glove convert converted according to all the nice proprieties for which some are ready to contend. Wouldn't it be a show?

All the conversions we have ever known were on the Zacchæus order: realizing such a need and feeling such a desire to come to Christ as to cause them to forget everything else and become oblivious to all that was conventional.

The Sycamore by the Wayside.

It seems as if that friendly old sycamore were put there by God himself for the special purpose of helping Zacchæus to see the Master. And there are God-planted sycamores all along the highway of human life designed to help men to get above the multitude and get a saving sight of the Son of God.

The inspired Word, the ordinances, special providences, the privilege of prayer and meditation—all these are as trees by the wayside by which we may climb above the throng. Who of us has not under the sermon, in the thoughtful reading, in the quiet of secret prayer risen above the things that press and crowd and clamor? How often by these means have we climbed up into a serener and quieter atmosphere, out of the material and into the sweet rest of the spiritual, and there above all else have we had glorious views of Christ!

He was to pass that way. Zacchæus knew that Christ was to pass that way, and hence he placed himself in position to intercept him. We know the points and places in life where he will pass. The path of duty, prayer, sacrifice, holy effort—these are the places which he will pass. He promises to meet us in those places. He will keep his word. He has said that our faith may pluck up a sycamore tree and transplant it in the sea; so our faith may transform our trials and misfortunes into sycamores, from whose branches we may gain a better and happier view of Christ. You will go from this service into the perplexities and temptations of the opening week. They will crowd you; you will be in the press. Then had you not better run before, get in advance, have such an adjustment of things that you may see the Master, commune with him, and know him better? Like Zacchæus, have him in your home and hear him say: "This day is salvation come to this house."

JONAH'S GOURD.

Text: "And God said to Jonah, Doest thou well to be angry for the gourd? And he said, I do well to be angry, even unto death." (Jon. iv. 9.)

HERE is the key to Jonah's character, and by using this key we find some ugly things in his make-up. But with it all he is a prophet of God. This may help some people to see what they never saw—how a man with weaknesses and ugly ways may be called of God to do his work. Some think that if a preacher is not perfect he has mistaken his calling and answered the call of some one else. Jonah's case answers this argument. He was full of defects, and yet God called him to be a prophet.

His Ingratitude.

Jonah was an ingrate, and the ingrate ranks among the high priests of meanness. God had selected him from all the men of his country to be his ambassador to one of the mightiest cities on earth, an honor that would perpetuate his name through all the ages. It was no excellency in Jonah that made him a necessity for this work. God could have found others fully as sweet-spirited and more obedient than he who would have gone direct to Nineveh without all that round-about route toward Tarshish and into the whale's belly and through the paths of the sea. But he left them in obscurity while he immortalized Jonah by making him his messenger. But for this he would never have been heard of outside his own precinct. He owed all to his commission, and we hear of him to-day simply because the word of the Lord came unto him. And here he is now, poor child of obscurity, in a desperate pout because God chose to glorify himself and spare Nineveh as it lay in sackcloth and ashes at his feet rather than glorify him by sweeping the city into destruction.

Here we have a typical grouch. Every character in Holy Writ is representative. Jonah here portrays one well known in pulpit and pew. Note those preachers who are always complaining that they are not appreciated, don't get the grade and promotion due them. You will find that they are like Jonah. They are men whom the Church has brought into notice, Church-made men. But for the reputation given us by the Church, some of us would never have been known farther than the back of the garden or the pea patch. The pew also has its representatives in this class. The mutterers in the Church are generally those who owe their standing and prominence to the Church.

His Deliverance.

His deliverance was the most wonderful in history, such as never was and never again will be. Yet he had so quickly forgotten it all! When those heathen sailors tossed him from their ship into the sea, to all human thought the hope of escape was folly. It would take the mad waters and the terrible sea monsters but a few brief moments to gulp or engulf the recreant prophet. But God was there. Admit God, and you have the solution of every problem. You ask me how the sea separated and let Israel pass over dryshod and then engulfed their enemies. I shall answer, God was there. You ask me how I have passed the narrow junctures in life where no human body could reach me. I answer, God was there. God is the answer to every question in his providence or in human destiny. Admit God, and there is no further question. God rode in that tempest as it chased that ship. His hand was upon the slimy head of that great fish and shielded the prophet from its terrible teeth as it gulped him down unhurt. God was with him in that living prison as he went down to the bottom of the mountains, while the bars of the earth were about him and the weeds were wrapped about his head.

His deliverance was as wonderful as his imprisonment. As he sat on the sand, fresh-belched from despair, and saw the monster sink back and disappear in the deep, it was no wonder that he shouted: "Salvation is of the Lord!" He shouted then that he would never forget his deliverance. But, strange to say, it is not yet forty days when we see this same man in a terrible temper and wanting to die. And what is the matter? Just two things: the great city is still living, and his pet gourd vine is dead.

Here is some of our moral ugliness. We have never been three days in the sea; but, like Jonah, we have been disobedient, and God has sent his agents after us to arrest us. When we were in dissipation, he sent nervousness and headache to correct us. When we abused our health, he sent disease to crush us down and pierce us with pains. When persisting in sin, he sent conscience with its double sting, and we have bled day and night under its torture. Again, without sin on our part, he has caused the waves and the billows to pass over us. A loved one was at death's door; you were in the deep, and the weeds were about your head and heart. You cried to God, and he sent deliverance, and the loved one lived. You have cried to him, and monster troubles have let you go and passed, like the monster from Jonah's sight, into the deep, and, like him, you have thought you would never forget this deed of the Lord's; yet how often since that have you been thrown into a pout over some trivial thing and been ready to murmur and complain!

Had Jonah as he sat under his gourd vine compared his condition with what it was inside that fish, his pout would have ended in a shout. When we are half sour and ready to murmur, we have only to recall God's deliverances and remember that we are living only because he interposed in a close juncture; then will gratitude take the place of grumbling, and pessimism will give way to praise.

He forgot God's forgiveness. He had sinned egregiously in refusing to obey God's command, and yet God forgave his disobedience. This he had forgotten and also the hour when he looked back upon the watery grave from which he had delivered him and shouted: "Salvation is of the Lord!" When God converted us, we thought we would never be done praising him; yet how shamefully and frequently have we forgotten all this! When your soul is ready to write bitter things, pause and think of your conversion, and the bitterness will pass. A thought of pardoning mercy will cure every complaint. He has forgiven enough to have sunk us to hell, and the reason we are in the Church and not in hell is because he has pardoned and not punished. Let the complainer think of how God forgave him and hide his head for very shame.

He forgot his success. I doubt if the preaching of any man since the world began was ever so successful as his. Noah's preaching was a failure compared with it. Even the ministry of the Master was not marked with such results. So soon as he began to preach the people began to repent. We have to preach for weeks to get a hearing and then preach a few more weeks to get the children and a few others to turn to God. Jonah hadn't preached three days before the king himself was on his knees in the dust. Then look at the city of six hundred thousand souls prostrate before God! The whole city was an altar of prayer and crowded with penitents. Everything was in sackcloth, from the king to the cattle. Was ever mortal man made such an instrument in God's hands? Now look at him in his booth watching the city on its knees before God, this illustrious mouthpiece of the Most High, there in full view of his six hundred thousand converts and in a fume and a fret and trying to die about a gourd vine. Did Holy Writ ever paint another such picture? And yet it is only a picture of that delectable thing we call human nature.

Many times have we sat for a picture like this. God has given you great and signal successes. In your suit for salvation Satan, the world, and your own evil nature were against you; but you gained the suit. God gloriously converted you. This was stupendous success. You brought a soul to Christ. This was success that an angel might envy. You reared your family in the fear of God. An archangel never equaled this. We have had a thousand successes; then we, after all, have often been ugly and fumed and fretted over the most trivial things.

The Question.

God said, "Doest thou well to be angry?"—that is, grieved and vexed. Jonah's sensibilities were a little mixed, his feelings were a little hurt, and at the same time he was a little mad. He hardly knew whether to curse or to cry. He felt like doing both. Haven't you sometimes had that feeling? Then it was so trivial a thing, only a gourd vine, and that not his! God made the vine and the worm to kill it. It was God's vine. It stood only for a day, but that was enough to turn Jonah's head. He was just as well off after it was dead as before it grew up, but he did not feel so. Give us a day's success, let some providential gourd vine spring up and spread its shade over us for a day and a night, then wither and leave us just where we were, and we get into a pout and almost wish to die. Some people never get over once being rich.

This gourd vine is typical. It pictures all our enterprises—a thing of comparative insignificance, like the things over which we do most fretting, little things in business, little things in society, little things in our fellow men, little things in everyday life. Such little vines are what we worry over most.

The Worm at the Root.

The worm was there, but Jonah didn't know it; only an inch or so under the surface, but he did not suspect it. There is a worm at the root of every earthly enterprise, a worm at the root of every vine, put there by God himself to measure its life and mark its fall. We cannot see an inch beneath the surface. We sit and rejoice in our pet schemes and know not that they are being silently cut down. The man builds on a foundation which a worm that builds lower than the skies may plow up.

"Doest thou well to be vexed for the gourd?" Thou whom God hath honored, whom God hath delivered from death, whom God hath so freely forgiven, to whom he hath given success, look back to-day over your life, as the prophet looked over the city he had won to God, while we ask again: "Doest thou well to be angry and grieved over the petty affairs of this life which grow up in a night and perish in a night?"

THE ANTIDOTE FOR TROUBLE.

Text: "Ye believe in God, believe also in me." (John xiv. 1.)

"YE believe in God." This is true of every man who has sense enough to be accountable. It was the fool who first said in his heart, "There is no God," and that idea is confined to his family unto this day. One of history employed a man to warn him daily of his mortality; but every man has a monitor within and a thousand monitors without, reminding him that there is a God. The breastworks of universal logic environ him and pour their resistless shots upon him from every point. The earth on which he stands, the heavens to which he looks, the atmosphere he breathes, all tell him of a God. The universe is a stupendous effect declaring a great first cause.

> "The spacious firmament on high,
> With all the blue ethereal sky,
> The spangled heavens, a shining frame,
> Their great Original proclaim.

> What though in solemn silence all
> Move round the dark terrestrial ball?
> What though no real voice or sound
> Amid their radiant orbs be found?
> In reason's ear they all rejoice
> And utter forth a glorious voice,
> Forever singing as they shine,
> 'The Hand that made us is divine.'"

The little child applies the smooth-lipped sea shell to its ear and, listening intently, catches the far-off murmur of the sea, telling of the mysterious union of that shell with the deep. This universe is the shell which to the ear of faith tells of its union with its great Creator.

Interior Evidence.

The proof of a God is not all exterior. When man looks in upon himself, he finds evidence that he cannot question, a hunger and a thirst which are more than mortal and call for food and drink, which are divine. Like the fin set for the water and the wing quivering for the air, man's undying nature pants for God. Thus with the proof pouring in from without upon his understanding and welling up from his moral nature within himself, he is compelled to believe in a God.

The man professing not to believe in a God is either insane or insincere. These two things, insanity and insincerity, make up the soul and body of atheism. All sane men believe in God and cannot help it, because the volume of evidence is as resistless as Niagara's thundering current.

But this does not bring peace. If the mere belief

in God's existence would bring peace, then this would be a peaceful world indeed. But this fact that there is a God only intensifies the unrest of the soul that is out of harmony with him. It is this faith forcing itself upon the sinner that doubles his wretchedness. If he could get rid of this and be satisfied that there is no God, his fears and forebodings would be far less. This is the trouble with men to-day; they can't get rid of God. This is the dreadful fact with every godless man; he cannot argue it away, nor laugh it away, nor ridicule it away, nor curse it away. This fact meets him at all points and at all times. It torments him with deliberation; it comes to him in his sinful indulgences; it appears before him ghostlike in the sleepless night hours; it haunts him everywhere; it arraigns him in the silent hours before the awful bar of his own conscience; and, as if not satisfied with present punishment, it points him away to a coming judgment and a future doom that cannot be written. The simple belief in God can produce nothing but discomfort in the sinner's mind; whereas if he could shake off this conviction he might have a partial relief. He can remove God's throne as easily as this fact.

The Remedy.

"Believe also in Christ." It is easier for men to believe in the greatness of God than in the goodness of God. They grasp the idea of his power much quicker than the idea of his love. Hence men are slow to believe in Christ because he is the expression of love rather than the expression of power. The leper said: "Lord, if thou wilt, thou canst make me clean." He believed in his power, but doubted his love. If Christ had been the expression of power, had he come as a conqueror to restore their nation, they (the Jews) would have owned and crowned him as their Messiah. Had the earth trembled under the tread of his power, the nations knelt at his feet, then they would have given him a throne and a crown rather than a cross and a sepulcher. Had he taught blood for blood, then they would have received him. But he taught, "Love your enemies," "Become as little children." Is this the Conqueror? Is this the Messiah who should loose our bonds? It is too much for the chaffing, panting Jew who had so long endured his bondage to Rome. Thus humanity still judges from its own standpoint. Christ is its abiding problem—so like it in person, so unlike it in character. Men look on him, as did Napoleon, and wonder yet hesitate to own him as Lord.

"Whom do men say that I, the Son of man, am?" This is the question of the ages, the question of to-day. Who is Christ? What shall I do with him? Where shall I place him? The one true answer came, and can only come, by inspiration: "Thou art the Christ, the Son of the living God." Flesh and blood did not reveal it. Brain power, labored logic, deep thinking will never solve this problem. It is too high for the mere understanding. It involves the heart. Hence it is by inspiration alone. The light and help of God are needed to see and place his Son upon his rightful throne in the soul.

This brings peace to the troubled heart. "Being justified by faith, we have peace with God through our Lord Jesus Christ." Here is perfect peace—peace that passeth understanding.

This removes the dread of God. There is an indescribable dread of God in the heart of the unbeliever. Nothing is more dreadful to him than the thought of meeting God. Man's first fallen impulse and effort were to get away from God. He hid himself. This is the world's impulse now. The ungodly even dislike to be where God's power is felt. They even dislike to talk of him. But to believe in Christ puts away this awful fear and dread. He becomes Immanuel. God is with us. God is in our thought, in our homes, in our lives, in our troubles.

This puts us on confident ground. Often we need the influence and intercession of a friend. I want employment. A man in large business can give it to me; but I do not know him. He is your friend. You can intercede for me. Christ intercedes for us, not for a place to work, but for a position where we may rule and reign and rest forever. Believing in Christ is putting your case into his hands. Making him your attorney, he has all power, all influence. He loves you well enough to undertake your case. He was never rejected with a plea. So to put your case in his hands is to be saved. It brings you upon confident ground, brings you upon the human side of the Godhead. Here we may come boldly.

Christ is the way. There was an inaccessible side to the city of God on Mount Zion where the perpendicular wall lifted itself to a dizzy height above the Valley of Hinnom. There was no access there, but there was access on the other side. The divine side to the kingdom of heaven is inaccessible. The Godhead in the abstract is too high and lifted up, too fearful in majesty, for our approach. But there is access on the other side, the human side, the Christ side. Coming around to that, we find that Christ is the way. To believe in God is to stand in Hinnom and look up at the inaccessible heights. To believe in Christ is to come around on the other side and enter in through the gates into the city.

See that impetuous Jew *en route* to Damascus struck down in terror and blindness! See that peaceful apostle yonder in prison and in sight of death writing his last message, "I am now ready to be offered"! Are they one and the same? Then why the difference? Yonder on the Damascus road he believed in God; here in the prison he believes in Christ.

Belief in Christ Frees from Inward Troubles.

Christ's troubles and sorrows were not his own. They were of the nobler and diviner sort. They arose out of his infinite unselfishness and infinite love. They were the sorrows of sympathy, the sorrows of compassion. A fallen world was drawing upon his moral feeling. He had the race on his heart. He groaned in spirit, but not for himself. He shed his blood, but not for his own sins. He was one with the Father, and beyond all his love burden and suffering was an ocean of peace and unapproachable glory; an ocean his disciples had never seen, though he hinted of this when he said: "I have meat to eat that ye know not of."

Here we find the place where we may hide the life

with Christ in God. It was out from this infinitude of glory that he came to seek for and to suffer for us. Noblest act of the eternities! When we come to believe in Christ, we enter in some sense into this retreat with him. Then when we come out from this joy, like him we come out to help and to suffer for others. It is necessary that we know the secret place of the Almighty before we are ready to help men.

The one in this retreat with Christ is little disturbed by life's storms. And even death is hailed with joy, since it conducts beyond the power of suffering and to where "the wicked cease to trouble, and the weary are at rest."

FIRST REAL ESTATE SALE.

Text: "Entreat for me to Ephron the son of Zohar, that he may give me the cave of Machpelah, which he hath, which is in the end of his field; for as much money as it is worth." (Gen. xxiii. 8, 9.)

FIRSTNESS has an undying charm. The first steamboat, the first locomotive, the first automobile, the first aëroplane—all have a novelty that is imperishable. Here we have the first recorded land sale. It is of such novelty and importance as to have minute record in Holy Writ, that we may see the entire transaction. It was a burial ground. This first land purchase was neither for a residence, a business block, nor a speculation. It was not selected as a country site, where this old prince of God might invest a portion of his wealth and spend life's evening time in luxurious ease; but this first sale is the sale of a cemetery.

Cain and Nimrod and Nebuchadnezzar built themselves cities, for their eyes were set toward the world, as the eye of Lot toward Sodom. But Abraham bought only a burial place. This was all the real estate he ever owned. He was never annoyed with false deeds, prior claims, State tax, nor public improvements. He had fine opportunity to be an extensive landholder. There were choice lands in Canaan then, and they were doubtless very cheap; but, like the mother who gives beauty, health, and life to rear a set of prodigal sons to crush her heart when her head is gray, Canaan gave birth to millions of Edomitish children, whom she nurtured at the cost of beauty, wealth, and power, while she is now a skeleton trodden under foot of her own wild and warlike offspring.

In Abraham's day Canaan was in her youth. The blush of beauty was on her vine-clad hills and fertile valleys. Abraham was rich and might have bought up those lands, as men do now, and made his family rich and left them lands to law over when he and Sarah were dead. In place of this he looked beyond and taught us a sublime lesson, thus declaring that he was a stranger and sojourner and would buy only a place to bury his dead; not to burn, but to bury his dead. (Cremation in its repulsiveness has no warrant or recognition in the Word of God.) This transaction stands as an undying rebuke to that avarice and greed of gain that is ever

"Stretching its arms like seas
To grasp in all the shores."

A Specimen of Religion in Business.

Religion is much more than many think. It is not the going regularly to some places and the staying away from others. It does not consist wholly in keeping out of bad company, saying prayers, hearing sermons, and putting in your contribution every Sunday. Religion does not use Sunday as a sort of clearing-off day in which to scour off the sins of the week. Genuine religion knows no difference in days, but so lives as to need no special Sunday sponging.

There is a common motto—and some mottoes are as full of poison as an African jungle is of dangers—"Business is business, and religion is religion." A thing may be just crooked enough so that it will not lie straight beside the Word of God or the Methodist Discipline. Not exactly correct or overhonest, but it is business. They all do it. It is custom. But custom does not make a wrong thing right. Custom commonizes sin, but cannot change its nature and make it other than sin. Religion meddles with a man's business, words, actions, plans, thoughts, and with his buying, selling commissions, profits—everything in his practical life.

It is a guardian angel. It is ever present and goes with a man to his store, office, and shop, as well as to his church and pew. It is the best angel in all the heavenly host. Think unkindly of another, and it whispers an apology. If you are about to say something severe, it puts its invisible hand on your lips and represses the sharp utterance. If we have done wrong, it thrusts a painful pin into the conscience. And these conscience pins are like fishhooks; they have barbs, and you cannot extract them. Poultice them as we may with apologies, still they hurt.

If you are selling a house and lot and there is a flaw

in the title or a defect in the property, that ever-present guardian will point it out. You may try for the time to forget it, but he brings all to your remembrance. If selling a piece of goods, it will make us tell the truth about its cost and show the shoddy that is in it. If selling fruit by the barrel, it will not let us put the small apples in the middle and bottom of the barrel and the large ones on top.

Sunday is least in the judgment. It is a mistake to conclude our final account a sort of Sunday reckoning, as if all depended upon what we do on Sunday. The truth is, Sunday is the day for not doing; it is the rest day. Sunday will be the least time factor in fixing our destiny. We are to be judged, not by the sermons heard, the songs sung, rituals repeated, prayers read, but by the deeds done in the body.

Our danger in the judgment is from the Mondays, Tuesdays, Wednesdays, Thursdays, Fridays, and Saturdays. Sunday is the day least to be dreaded. Many of us could go to heaven on a Sunday record. Sunday shuts the avenues of busy life, hushes the babble of the commercial multitudes, takes us out of the way of a thousand chances to do wrong, and bids us sit down and think on higher and holier things.

Circumstances of This Sale.

"He went to the gate." There was the place where the officials sat and where such business was transacted, and there in the most public manner he made his proposition. He didn't get some shyster to inquire around on the sly and find out if Ephron was in a tight place and compelled to have a little ready money, then offer him cash down, about half of what his ground was worth; but he said: "Speak to Ephron, that he give me the property for as much money as it is worth."

He knew nothing of that sort of sympathy (?) that hunts for a man under pressure, hurries to him and kindly furnishes a little money for present relief, then takes a deed to his home, leaving him and his family without shelter. We once knew a feat like this performed by a prominent Churchman. This is a sort of raven sympathy. The raven is a very sympathetic bird. When it finds the unfortunate lamb down and helpless and about ready to die, it will kindly pick out its eyes, the sooner to put it out of pain.

Seeking to get goods and chattels at less than value produces a sort of commercial cannibalism and sets men eating up each other. This is at the base of that fraudulent spirit that has become universal—ignoring the principle of the grand old patriarch, "that he give me the property for as much money as it is worth."

It is a matter of supply and demand. We complain at the frauds that flood the land, and yet we create the demand. There is a mighty demand and hence a vast supply. The spirit of the age is to get things for less than their value. If a man sells largely, he must undersell. To undersell and sell largely he must adulterate. The demand is for bargains, and hence the adulteration that can furnish bargains. Buy an article at half value, and the neighbor's first question is, "Where did you get it?" He goes at once to that store and notifies others, and soon there is a rush and crush, simply because everybody wants something for less than it is worth. This generates dishonesty through the whole commercial realm. This is what builds cheap-John stores, ninety-nine-cent stores, five-cent stores, misfit counters, hangs "Bankrupt Sale" signs over the doors, and puts job lots in the front windows and falsehood in a thousand forms through the whole system of trade.

No branch of commerce is exempt. It puts ocher in your house paint and rotten wood in your buggy wheels, chemicals in your groceries, and shoddy cloth in your clothing. And as if it were not enough to be the cheapest place uptown, it paints itself on the grocery wagons and on the back of a negro and sends them through the town, living and moving epistles of fraud, to be seen and read of all men. Hence the whole mercantile system is one vast whited sepulcher, and why? Because we demand it. The world is bound to have things for less money than they are worth.

Abraham maintained his self-respect. He had made his impress upon those sons of Heth, as every man of God will on those about him. They offered to give him a burial place, but he stood up and bowed himself before them. Old and infirm, he was still the grand old gentleman. Hence the most finished manner and courtesy characterize him in this transaction. Courtesy and right-bearing are a part of religion. "It doth not behave itself unseemly." No office, eminence, or ability can ever place a man where he may ignore the finer proprieties or the delicate courtesies due his fellow man. That which gave gloss to the character of Abraham will give an attraction and beauty to all in every rank and station in life.

Abraham recognized their generosity, but would neither put himself under obligation to them nor run the risk of some minor heir of Ephron raising a future claim to the ground. Here is an example of prudence in business with self-respect maintained through the entire transaction. He also paid cash for his purchase. Blessed is the man who can pay cash for what he gets! "He weighed out the money current with the merchant." No questionable currency, no dross in the metal. He then received the conveyance, the field with all its appurtenances. Here we have religion and business and religion in business, correct in principle as it is exalted in morals.

Location of This Purchase.

It was "in the end of the field." Here is human life. Let our field of labor or experience be what or where it may, fair and fertile as Goshen's valleys or rugged and barren as the sides of Sinai, whether there be fruits and flowers or barrenness and destitution, like the field of Ephron, there is a sepulcher at the end of the field. We are fagging through that field to-day, struggling on toward our own Machpelah at the end. We must plod through heat and cold, sunshine and shadow until we reach the border where our grave is in waiting.

It was a permanent possession. Abraham held his claim and holds it yet, and the field bought that day still holds his dust and that of his dead. The sepulcher is the most enduring possession. It is the next step to immortality and, like it, the most enduring. This transaction has stood through the ages and has never been annulled—typical of resurrection rights. Machpelah is his, and he shall claim his own in the final day. Our graves are our own. Let there be upheaval, change, revolution, and wreck; yet the dust of our dead shall be ours in the final awakening. Christ has bought our burial place for us. He paid the full price and has given us the guarantee that because he lives we shall live also.

THE MAJESTY OF MAN.

Text: "What is man, that thou art mindful of him?" (Ps. viii. 4.)

GOD'S mind is full of man. This declares his majesty. A creature that fills the mind of God cannot be of less than supreme import. What is man? Vast stores of rhetoric and logic have been expended in the effort to answer this question. Efforts have been made to make man express himself, tell what he is by what he has done. You might as well try to make a machine explain itself. The explanation lies back with the one who invented it.

A creature can neither understand nor explain itself. To do this would argue the wisdom of a creator. Self-comprehension implies Godhead. God is the only being in the universe who is a true exponent of himself. Trying to show what man is by what he has done is simply absurd.

Man has had no chance. Were it even possible for him to express himself, he has been without opportunity. He is under the blight of sin and paralyzed in his higher powers. His only perfect opportunity was in Eden, and that as transient as a sunbeam through a cloud rift. His life since that has been cut to a span. His cradle and his coffin almost touch. He has not had so much as a single century for experience. The mind has but budded and experience shown its first faint tints of ripeness when the curtain drops, the bell tolls, and the drama is ended.

The giants of the Yosemite, with earth and air congenial and a thousand years for growth, lift their heads four hundred feet heavenward, grand illustrations of what time and opportunity can do. Suppose some giant soul could have a thousand years for development; who could tell its moral altitude and power? But to offer what man has done, under his disabilities, as an expression of what he is, is unjust to him and a reflection on the God who made him.

God's investment is the answer. If you would know what man is, note what God has invested in him. He makes no mistakes, no unwise or unprofitable investments. He knew what man would cost before he made him. He knew tthe misfortunes in his history before that history began.

"Many, O Lord, are thy wonderful works, and thy thoughts which are to usward." God's thoughts, back of his works, are "to usward."

The child learns its own significance as it studies the plans of its father laid out for it. Man will rightly estimate himself as he studies what God has planned for him. If you would know yourself, study the divine. Man was last in creation, but first in the divine thought. The universe was planned with reference to man. God did not make a cage and then seek a songster to fit the cage; he did not build a world and then make a creature to fit the building; but his thoughts were usward. All the stupendous work was in view of man. God's framing thoughts and building thoughts and starry thoughts and growing thoughts and rolling sea thoughts all were toward man. Mark the flow of this sea tide of God's thoughts, see it as it breaks upon the shores of human destiny, and learn what is man.

Creation is ever loyal to man. Cursed and suffering for man's sake, yet it remains true to him, like the loyal slave in the Revolutionary War when his master's home was burned by the British. He lay concealed near by and suffered his body to be blistered by the flames and when discovered preferred to be hung up by the neck rather than betray his master. Creation, scarred and abused because of man's sin, still clings to him and suffers with him.

The skies retain their cerulean softness, so soothing to the aching eyes as they look heavenward. The sun seems as if he had only come down a part of the way from glory to give us an intimation of the unapproachable effulgence, and yet it comes not too near, lest we be unable to bear it. I see the cloud gather and feel the earth quiver as heaven's draft horses move with thunderous tread, bringing the watery burden to refresh the thirsty land. I see the fierce lightnings cross swords in the skies, the storm angels bearing the torches that burn the subtle death from the air we breathe. Look downward, and earth is silently unrolling the carpet of velvetlike grass and flowers, as the bride's walk way, that our steps may go softly on life's way. Earth anticipates man's wants, feeds him with the richest of her fruits and the finest of her wheat; and when in weariness he falls upon his final sleep, she takes him to her bosom, where he is nursed in restful silence until he wakes refreshed in eternity's morning dawn. Creation's trend, like the thought of God, is to usward.

Redemption.

This is a deeper investment. We go back into the heart of God to find it. Man is a sufferer. God in redemption became a sufferer and lays his suffering beneath man's suffering. He takes all the weight of man's stupendous curse.

The Gulf Stream is the mighty equalizer in the realm of the deep. Majestic in volume, flowing through the heart of the ocean, it gives out from its warm current the influences which modify extremes and give beauty and blessing to every shore. Still its work is noiseless, the silent force in the sea, and is known by the influence wafted upon the world.

Redemption is the gulf stream from the heart of God flowing through the ages. It gives out its warmth in the cold sea of human life, making it joyous, springing verdure and beauty in the midst of barrenness, and putting a smile on the sad face of a fallen world.

Education.

God's investment is as marked in man's education as in his creation and redemption. Kings seek for their sons the most renowned preceptors, though royalty never condescends to teach. But here divine royalty becomes teacher; the Holy Ghost comes to teach and lead us into all truth. Where God is preceptor the pupil cannot be less than royal.

The general who leads a campaign has but one aim; that is victory. He captures, conscripts, confiscates, demolishes, does all that contributes to conquest. The Holy Ghost as our Leader presses all into service to one great end. Misfortune, loss, grief, and disappointment, all serve him. We put on crape, wring the hands, sit in ashes, and weep over desolation. All this is but a part of the warfare to bring us into eternal freedom and rulership.

What is man? See what God has invested, how he is handling him. The tides of his thought, the gulf stream of his love, the processes of his education are all flowing toward man. He can but look up and cry: "Tell me, O my Father, what I am."

Earthliness of Men.

While God invests all, how little do men care for themselves! Left without divine influence, their trend is downward, earthly, sensual, devilish. A prize fight will prove this. With all the moral enginery of high civilization and the influences from the gulf stream of grace, the thought of ninety millions of people has been given for days to the mutual butchery of two human brutes, lower than the Spanish bullfight, a blood-and-beef slugging between two human bulls. The public press was full, the highway was full, the homes were full of the spirit of the thing, and the very tots waking in the morning had to know who whipped before they were dressed.

The Church is of the same spirit, only a little changed by grace, and sometimes only a little. I saw a notice of a coming camp meeting, with men to preach for the multitudes, the wittiest, most entertaining men of the age, holding their hearers with the most side-splitting puns and irresistible humor. Has it come to this? Has the gospel degenerated into an entertainment and its success dependent upon the wit and humor of its heralds?

Look at the lands beyond the sea, after ages of education and higher culture, which have drawn our students by the thousands. See them now at each other's throats and using means of destruction so hellish as to make the savage blush for shame. And as if nothing yet was sufficiently fiendish, they are now contemplating bombs loaded with germs of the most deadly plague to be dropped from the air upon their enemies. One thing this unprecedented war will demonstrate: that neither education nor anything else can save men or nations—nothing except the transforming power of the gospel of Christ.

Man's Destiny.

This is the best definition of man. The dove let loose from the ark went out but to return. No rest for her foot was found, and she "waited yet other seven days." When we seek to explore the future, the mind, dovelike, grows weary and returns, content to wait yet other days until the tops of the eternal hills are visible. Then may we leave this ark of clay to return no more.

Our destiny is the grandest conception touching our being. We gain as we advance. Each investment augments our significance. I can conceive of a time when things shall not be as now—ocean dry, rocks crumbled, sun faded, earth consumed. I can conceive of a time when I was not, but I can conceive of no time when I shall not be.

The Christian man may look upon his family circle and say within himself: "These shall be with me a thousand ages hence." There are vacant chairs in almost every home. Death has separated my children from me; but, like the child Jesus, separated three sorrowful days from his parents, I shall find them, as they found him, in the temple.

This destiny is an eternal ascension; this blood-washed family is a part of the escort of the Son of God in his tour of the eternities; here to-day, to-morrow with God. A thousand years hence it is just beginning to know God's investment in man. We look back and wonder at our creation, redemption, and education; but we go forward for destiny alone to answer the question, "What is man?"

Drafts on the Unseen.

Text: "Whereby are given unto us exceeding great and precious promises." (2 Pet. i. 4.)

A PROMISE is a pledge of future good, and its value is in proportion to its magnitude and the character of its author. There is a vast difference between a county bond and a United States bond. We have real property in promises according to size and solidity.

Design of the Divine Promises.

We are neither what nor where God ultimately wants us to be. He is seeking to lift us from the natural to the supernatural. The heritage in store for us cannot be shoved down into this narrow state. Hence he would enlarge us and bring us up to the inheritance. The promises guarantee the future good and thus become a property to us.

I employ a laborer, but give him nothing in advance. He goes to the toil, but sees no reward. My promise is his hope. It nerves him to labor, and he works by faith. God's promises are all that is in sight to us. We see no angel nor any outline of heaven, no far-off light. We see nothing but his promise; that makes the unseen real. They are "the substance of things hoped for, the evidence of things not seen." These bonds on the divine government are interest-bearing, and their interest is equal to life's emergencies. The coupons are neither annual nor semiannual, but daily. They mature day by day, and by them we have our daily bread.

They are the only safe property. A man sells home and farm and appurtenances and invests all in United States bonds. He gives all that is visible for a simple pledge from the government. Thus when a man turns to God he sells all, renounces the world, parts with the things that are seen, and takes God's promise for the things that are not seen.

We get an idea of values when we compare our

property in the promises with our best material property. Real estate is our very best. It cannot be stolen, burned up, or destroyed. Our lands are fire-proof, burglar-proof, and rust-proof. But are they fraud-proof? Fraud can do what flood or fire cannot do. It can find a flaw in the title, bring up and establish a long-buried claim, or hatch out a new claim at the point of pretended law upon the possession you vainly called your own.

There were Southern homes at the outbreak of the Civil War, residences of landed lords, princely palaces, that would command fabulous figures. Four short years swept away their beauty and value and left them as worthless as the untamed lands of the West.

My first land investment was taken from me by a prior claim. But God's freeholders through the promises are in no danger of such happenings. I have no such fear where I am now investing. There are no prior claims. Our titles run back beyond possibility of loss. The abstracts not only run back to the patentee, but back to Him who made the property and gave us the deeds. By Him were all things made. These divine deeds don't come to us second-hand nor fourth-hand nor ten-thousand-hand, but direct from Him who made it and who says: "It was prepared for you."

The elements affect all material properties. Our best possessions are subject to the caprice of the clouds. The landlord may cultivate on a princely scale, and the most ethereal elements may blight him. If the clouds decline to water his fields and the air grows hot and angry, his farms blister, his stock perishes, and he sits a pauper with his desk full of deeds; and all because the winds and the clouds refused to sign his papers and make his income sure. What ownership has he, after all, unless God makes the elements indorse his claim?

But the promises lie up above the capricious air currents. They originate away back of the uncertain clouds; they are the same in famine or in plenty; they are deeper than the rain fountains, as good in Sahara as in the well-watered plains, as valid under the juniper as on Carmel.

See Moses yonder at Horeb, famishing Israel at his feet, crying, clamoring, cursing, their very tongues stiff and cleaving to the roofs of their mouths. The heavens are brass, the sun a furnace; there is no cloud the size of a hand on the horizon. But look! He has the promises of God, and they never dry up. They live where vegetation is parched and dead. See, he rests upon them, strikes the hot and dusty rock, and the cool waters gush as clear as crystal out of the promise, independent of sky or cloud or air. The skies may mock and the winds tantalize, but they are drinking, drinking, dipping it with the cups of the promises, and looking up to laugh at the elements over which they have triumphed. This is what is meant by promises "exceeding great and precious"; promises that carry a man up above nature, up where nature has put him down, like Ishmael under the bramble, and left him to die; promises that take him up in the extreme hours and give him water out of the rock at noonday and bread out of the skies at night.

The promises are always redeemable. You may

have drafts for a million and be in a strange land where you can neither negotiate nor discount them, and you may die of want with all your claims. But you can cash the promises anywhere and at any time. They are payable not in somebody's bank, but anywhere in the universe of God, in heaven or on earth. They are payable anywhere except in hell. God redeems nothing there, transacts no business, nor has so much as a branch office in hell. But anywhere out of hell and at any hour you have the privilege to present and have his promise honored.

There are no set hours. The banks in your town transact no business on the streets nor in the bank between certain hours; but God's promises are cashed anywhere, at any time, in the wilderness or in the street, on the land or on the sea, at noonday or at midnight, at the marriage altar or the bed of death, in the furnace or in the den, in the whirlwind or in the whale's belly. The gates of grace are never closed. The lock is not set to a certain hour. You don't have to wait. God's banking hours are from midnight to midnight and from sun to sun.

Why need we wait? Must our God have time to gather up his forces to meet our drafts? Is he unable to be generous? I have known men whose generosity drove them into bankruptcy. Will God's infinite goodness exhaust his resources? Must he wait to answer us? Must the winds gather force to waft the thistledown, or the ocean gather power to toss a feather, or the sun bring up his resources to dry a dewdrop? Then may our God have to wait before taking our burden or drying our tears. He is infinite in resources and eternally real. Now is his supreme moment. He fills the past and the future, but acts in the present. The eternal activities play into the now of time, sublime focal point, God's opportunity and man's possibility, the point where the two meet in unison, the point of salvation, the greatest day in human history. Time past is time in its tomb, time to come is time unborn; and he is only less than a lunatic who depends upon the buried or the unborn. Then turn to God now. To-day is the day and only day of salvation.

Firmness of the Promises.

A promise is worth just the ability and integrity which are back of it. We care nothing for the promise of some men because they are without character and too mean to keep their word. Others we know whose promise would be worthless because they have nothing with which to pay. God's promises rest upon his purity and power. Infinite purity and infinite power prop them. They cannot fail while God's character remains unchanged.

"Firm as his throne his promise stands." His resources are pledged. He makes no reserve. No hint of a reserve has ever been detected in his dealings with us. He gave himself and now pledges all that he represents to stand good for us.

How to Use the Promises.

We must love them as the miser loves his gold. I know an old woman who had a few thousand dollars in United States bonds. I have seen her as she would sit for hours handling those bonds and counting the coupons while her heart rested upon them. Thus are we to love and handle and daily count the coupons on those exceeding great and precious bonds on the Unseen. "They are sweeter than honey and the honeycomb." The comb may drop some sweetness of itself; but handle and press it, and you get the flow. Squeeze and press the promises with the miser's devotion, and you get their full sweetness. The grapes left on the vine will not exhilarate; but gathered and pressed, they yield the wine that makes glad the heart. God's grapes must not be left on the inspired vine, but we must gather and press and drink their soul-cheering juices. They are ripe at all seasons. It is always the time of the gathering of grapes in this vineyard of the Lord. But, alas! the taste for these heavenly fruits is often destroyed by indulgence in the trashy sweets of the world.

Learn to wait on the Lord. While he always cashes our drafts for present needs, we must learn to wait for the future good. The maple buds in the early springtime, while the mulberry remains unchanged and is late and last to put forth its leaves; yet we do not get impatient waiting for the mulberry. Some of God's promises are speedily fulfilled, while others are later in the life season. Haven't we had some promises fulfilled? Haven't we had the early almond and the maple in bloom? Then can we not wait on the mulberry promises? They will bloom in season, later on in life, but at the proper time. If the trees never bloom out of time, will his promises ever fail in their time?

The promises are the pavement for the life walk—

broad, deep, everlasting, exceeding great. Yet we hesitate and totter as if walking the slender wire; whereas we ought to run and leap and laugh and rejoice, his word beneath us, his grace our supply, connection with his throne at all points and at all hours. As in the street car, we have only to lift the hand and pull the bell. God's promises, like the car straps, dangle about us. And while I must rise to reach the car strap, I need not rise to pray, but simply lift the faith hand and grasp the promise. Life with the child of God is a street car excursion, and the promises are ever in reach.

USE WHAT WE HAVE.

Text: "What is that in thine hand?" (Ex. iv. 2.)

THIS was God's question to Moses when he hesitated to undertake to liberate the children of Israel. To attempt the release and removal of two millions of slaves from the mightiest empire on earth would certainly require force and equipment which he was sure he did not have. He was not in a state of "preparedness." But his weakness is made the background for the manifestation of God's power. He will prove to Moses that he has all that is needed for this stupendous undertaking. We are always in the majority when God is on our side. Hence he shows Moses that the implement and emblem of power is now in his hand.

He called him as a shepherd. So he will empower him as such. He did not require him to go and learn the use of a bow or a battering-ram, but made the simple instrument with which he was familiar to be the implement of his power. The rod was a part of his shepherd equipment. He was never without it. It was that with which he tended his flock and on which he leaned when weary. Now, God will make it the protection of his flock as Moses leads them out from their bondage. The rod was a thing familiar to all shepherds. There was not one on the plains or on the hilltops who was not as well equipped in the practical sense as was Moses. Each carried in his hand an implement like that of Israel's leader.

God uses men as they are. He takes them with such qualifications as they have. Moses might have stood and said: "I have nothing but this insignificant rod. I can do nothing, because I have nothing to do it with."

Some men are doing nothing because they have not great gifts or great fortune. God does not call for fortune or genius, but asks: "What is that in thine hand?" What have you at your command? What, however insignificant? Use that. You may have no power beyond your own home circle. All your force may be in the labor of your hands. Then wield that for God.

How did the rod become powerful? When handled as God directed, it became a living thing of power. In the presence of the king it was an all-conquering serpent that swallowed up the serpents of the magicians. Its stroke filled the land with lice and covered the earth with frogs to plague Egypt. Its motion parted the waters to let Israel pass over and closed them again to destroy their pursuers. When they were famished for water at Horeb, the stroke of this rod brought forth the cooling stream.

The same God that put life in that old rod will put life and power into the commonplace things with which we are connected. Every life, however obscure, becomes powerful when lived for God. Every man is a power who handles his life as God directs. Pharaoh felt that shepherd's crook when it fell a living, fiery serpent at his feet.

Then what have you in your hand? Is it a painter's brush, a mason's trowel, a teacher's ferrule, a grocer's balance, or a merchant's yardstick? Whatever it may be, so handle it that it may impress the gainsayers. Let it be so in league with God that men may feel its moral force. That old rod was not the only thing that ever carried God-given power. He puts moral power into every implement his servants handle. We have only to take heed to what is in our hands and handle it for God. Let it be known that a man is honorable and consecrated to God, and there is a gospel power in his very business house. You go into his place of business with that pleasant, trustful feeling with which you enter the church, conscious that you will not be defrauded, but may safely rely on all that is there. There is a conscious restfulness in this and a moral power not easily defined.

What is in your hand as a parent? More than a shepherd's crook, a mason's trowel, or a grocer's gauge. You have the destiny of children, dearer than all things else. You are training the scions of future citizenship, the infant men, who will man the State and mold the morals of the land forty years hence.

What you make your children now they will make society and the Church when you, like Isaac, are on the couch of helpless age. As surely as you plant the trees in the shade of which your children will rest, so surely will you implant in them the principles which will give coloring to the morals of your country in coming time.

Shall your children make history? Shall they stand before kings? Shall they smite the dry rocks in life's famished places and draw forth living waters? Shall they, when defeat seems evident, divide the waters and pass the apparent impossibilities on the life march? Then let them be given to God in childhood. Get them in league with him while they are young and let God handle them. Then will they make history for you when you are gone. The future of this nation—its honor, its virtue, and its exaltation—is in your hands as the parents of the future citizenship.

What is in your hand as a candidate for immortality? The opportunities of life. These are as completely in your power to manipulate and use as was the rod in the hand of Israel's leader. But, like the rod, they are so commonplace that we miss their value. Our opportunities are ever with us; they are part of life's equipage, and yet we regard them of no great significance and give them little thought.

Each season has its lessons and opportunities. The man of fifty has passed two hundred seasons. Each day in that time had its opportunities, and there have been nearly twenty thousand of those days. In one pastorate of four years there are two hundred prayer meeting hours, two hundred Sunday school hours, and four hundred hours for preaching and hearing the gospel. Add to these the special occasions, and you have almost a thousand services in one pastorate. Passing, as many do, through ten such pastorates, you have almost ten thousand presentations of the gospel in a lifetime. That power is put in your hand almost ten thousand times, and yet, like Moses holding the rod in his hand, regarding it a thing of small moment, or rather not thinking of it at all! Thus we pass our opportunities daily without thought of their immense worth. Moses had never thought that the rod, so familiar to him, was to appall kings, divide seas, and triumph over enemies.

What things are now in your hand—things unnoticed, unappreciated, uncared-for! And yet these are the things, the very things, that will decide destiny, determine the future, and settle the final doom.

Moses fled when he saw the serpent. When he saw the power and the danger that were in the rod that he had regarded as so insignificant, he fled from it in dismay. The touch of God showed him what was in it. So with the opportunities that men handle, abuse, and waste. Could they but see their awful meaning and the tremendous issues which hang upon them, they would tremble and fly from them.

Those long-abused and neglected opportunities will under God's touch and in the dying hour become living, fearful, fiery serpents, and the helpless, hopeless soul would fain fly from them. But, alas! the soul will then be in their grasp, and flight will be impossible.

What is in your hand in personal influence? Here

is a rod of power of which we seldom think. Our mightiest work is done by your influence. Yet we know not what we do. Influence is from "influo," to flow in, the silent inflow of an element, the inflow of our power upon the hearts, lives, and characters of others. We thus flow in upon others until they become what we make them, what we are.

We carry this rod of power all the time and think of it as little as Moses thought of the rod until God touched it. We make men do and they make us do what neither law nor money nor bribes nor aught else could make us do. May God show us what power we have in our personal influence!

"In Thy Hand."

Not merely in view, in prospect, in possibility, but in your hand, at command, even as the rod in the hand of the shepherd. Do not say: "I have no influence." A shepherd is not a shepherd without his crook. A man is not a man without influence. As a parent, as a candidate for immortality, as one with personal influence, I ask: "What is that in thine hand?" May the living God show us the powers we hold and for which we shall give account as we have never seen them before! May they be used for him, and used now, ere they become serpents and take the form of the worm that dieth not and make conscience to become their deathless victim!

COMING TO TERMS.

Text: "Agree with thine adversary quickly, whiles thou art in the way with him; lest at any time the adversary deliver thee to the judge, and the judge deliver thee to the officer, and thou be cast into prison. Verily I say unto thee, Thou shalt by no means come out thence, till thou hast paid the uttermost farthing." (Matt. v. 25, 26.)

WHO is the adversary? Whatever may be the primary meaning here, God is the adversary of sin. God hates sin. God will ultimately destroy all sin and all souls who refuse to renounce it. But redeeming love holds divine wrath in abeyance, while God himself comes as a plaintiff with a complaint against the sinner and seeks to bring him to agreement with himself. So the adversary becomes the plaintiff.

The word is not "confer" nor "compromise," but "agree" with him, come to his terms, comply with his requirements. Here is a distinctive feature of the gospel. Salvation is one price. Other things may be marked down and may fluctuate in price with the seasons, but the price of pardon is without change. Some pulpits mark it down, but the marked-down salvation, like shoddy goods, will not wear and last. A genuine, all-gold pardon is never to be had for less than an absolute agreement with God.

Agree with him quickly. There is need of haste. Issues are involved which admit of no delay or indifference, something of such moment as to allow no claim before it. This word "quickly" should fill the unsaved soul with alarm. It is a danger signal. We use it at the tragic moments, when the flames burst through the dwelling, when the dead one is in danger, when life hangs upon a moment. This is the word used to urge the sinner to agreement with God. It is a moral volcano. God himself is using it and urging haste.

"While thou art in the way with him." God has come to save the lost. He travels with every man in the first stages of life for the express purpose of bringing him to an agreement and into harmony with himself.

Sinner, you have a divine traveling Companion. Whether you realize it or not, God is journeying with you. Your life may be to him an incessant insult, yet he follows you with more than a father's solicitude. The plan of salvation is simply God's devisement to get into the way with us and journey with us for a time. This life, therefore, is the most momentous part of our existence. Brief it is, but fraught with destiny. How solemn, how awful is life! How tremendous its issues!

His walk with us reveals his character. When one has sinned against us, we are slow to propose adjustment, if indeed we do it at all; but God comes to us seeking to reconcile us. How can he afford it? You say: "I cannot afford to go to my enemy and offer terms of friendship." How, then, can God afford it? He could not if he had as little right character as we have. But such is his wealth of character that he can afford it. So vast is the difference between God and us that he can afford this approach and offer to us.

You feel no resentment toward the little child when it is angry and rebellious, but you seek to quiet and comfort its spirit. But if the parent of that child offends you, you resent the offense. Why is this? The parent has character, while the child has not.

In our smallness of character God deals with us as we deal with the little child, and he does it simply because he is God and infinitely above us in nature and character. We also see his infinite patience daily in the life journey. When we propose to compromise with an enemy, we do not wait long for his reply. If he says, "I will think over this matter; come back to see me again," we do not parley with the ignoble creature. And we could see him in the neighborhood of the last river before we would go to him again. But God has such grace and character that he comes to us again and again and even stands at the door of the heart and knocks for admission.

"Lest he deliver thee to the judge." Among the Orientals the creditor had power to arrest and arraign the debtor. God is the great Creditor, who has the sinner at his mercy. He can bear with him or deliver him to judgment by his own sovereign power and will. Hence as he travels with us *en route* to the judgment let us wisely redeem the time and agree with him quickly.

The Judge.

It is the office of the judge to pass sentence and fix doom. Here we have the impersonation of that white-haired skeleton form whose jurisdiction is universal and whose scepter is a scythe. We call him "death." All flesh and all spirits out of harmony with God shall pass under his dominion. The body of the saint will come under his power, but his spirit has the victory over death, while the sinner is delivered, soul and body, into his hands.

Death is such a judge as has no sympathy. He knows no clemency. Pity is a term at which he sneers and claps his skeleton hands in derision. He knows no bribes and changes no decisions. But God will break his power over the very dust of his saints, while the impenitent will rise only to pass into the second death.

"And the judge deliver thee to the officer." The officer inflicted the punishment, applied the bastinado or other instrument of torture. Satan stands as the ready servant of death. As the angels do the will of God in heaven, devils do the will of death in hell. To be delivered by the judge to the officer is to pass under doom from the hand of death into the custody of Satan and by him to be cast into prison.

The Prison.

Hell is the great universal state prison of the damned. We build prisons, one or more, and they prove too small; but the prison of the universe is ample in capacity. Not built within but outside the corporation of God's domain—built without, where there is room, infinite room, eternal room. Outer darkness, out where the sun never shines nor the stars ever smile, out where God himself never looks. Outer darkness is the prison. The effort to escape it is but to plunge deeper. Were it walled in or circumscribed, then might one escape. But its very outerness is its impregnability. To go farther is to sink deeper into its gloom. Outer darkness! Who can portray it?

Autobiography of Bishop Henry Clay Morrison.

At Any Time.

Here is royal prerogative. The issues of life are in his hands; not at a suitable time nor an appointed time, but at any time. No moment is exempt. Nature has her set times. Her flowers bloom, her fruits ripen, her snows fall in their appointed seasons. But death walks side by side with man from his cradle, his skeleton form keeping step with his step and his scythe just in his advance, at midnight or at noon, in pleasure's round or sorrow's depths, when least expected or least prepared—at any time.

Who die just when they expect it? Raphael's greatest painting was left unfinished on the easel. The merchant's daybook is left half posted on his counter. The books of the schoolboy (as in my own home) lie strapped and buckled under his desk, laid down at evening time, never to be taken up. At this moment the invisible archer may be poising the arrow and bending his bow with unerring aim at some one in this audience. At any time!

The Prison Term.

"Until thou hast paid the uttermost farthing." In the British National Gallery is the celebrated picture of Perseus holding up the head of Medusa. That head turned every one into stone who looked upon it. There is a warrior with a dart in his hand. He stands stiffened into stone. Another with a poniard beneath his robe and just ready to strike, but he is now an assassin in statue, motionless and cold. Another creeping stealthily with murderous intent, but there he stands in stone. He looked upon that fatal head, only to be instantly petrified.

Such is death. What I am when I look upon it I shall be forever. If I see death in bad character, I shall be transfixed in that character. Death sets the character colors and makes them as changeless as eternity. O the duration of the doom in outer darkness! "Until I have paid the uttermost farthing."

How shall I pay a debt so vast that Christ could only meet it with the blood of his heart? But O the wonder of his love! He will pay, he has paid, all our hopeless debt, and now he only asks that we accept what he has done, that we agree and come into harmony with him. Then while you may accept release from this mountain load, this burden of sin which will sink you eternally, accept that deliverance now. Agree with him now, agree with him quickly, lest at any time—to-day, to-night, to-morrow—he deliver thee to the judge, and the judge deliver thee to the officer, and thou be cast into the prison eternal.

BROKEN CISTERNS.

Text: "For my people have committed two evils; they have forsaken me the fountain of living waters, and hewed them out cisterns, broken cisterns, that can hold no water." (Jer. ii. 13.)

OUR blessings are so manifold and continuous that we lose appreciation and forget their value. In this land of rains and rivers, fountains and hydrants we forget the worth of water. But the people of Jeremiah's day and land knew its value. There it rained but twice in the year. Cisterns were digged, filled, and then concealed to save family and flock from famishing in the summer's drought. In place of water flowing into marble basins in every room the women with rope and pitcher trudged to and from the well, however distant, to carry water for the family supply. "Come unto me," said the Nazarene, "and I will give you rest." And the nations which have come to Christ have found rest, have put away their well ropes and water pitchers, while steam and electricity are doing the work for them. Women have quit the care of field and flocks and are queens in their Christian homes.

The elevation of women and the mitigation of labor for man and beast mark the march of our Christianity. The home is sweeter, the fields more productive, and the very brutes are happier where Christ reigns.

The Two Evils.

They turned away from God and sought the world. This is ever true: in proportion as the hold on God is loosed, the grasp is made tighter upon the world. The soul has just so much grasping power and is incapable of a firm grasp on two objects at the same time. You cannot look closely at two things at the same moment. You cannot listen attentively to two conversations at the same time. So we cannot serve God and Mammon at the same time. If the soul has a living grasp upon God, it will hold the world very lightly, and it is little trouble to let the world go; whereas if the grasp be firm upon the world the hold on God will be correspondingly feeble. There is no middle notch in the moral scale beam to bring it to a horizontal rest. You cannot force a hoop upon a vessel when hoop and vessel are the same size. Force the hoop down at one point, and it flies up at another. The hoop must be larger than the vessel.

Our love to God must be larger than our love for the world, otherwise life can never be religiously symmetrical. Life with many is a constant effort to force on the small hoop. They never get all parts of the character into compass. If they succeed in one direction, there is a bulge in another. A man's religion must be all-inclusive, large enough to encompass his entire being and nature. The beautiful life is large and broad and sufficiently Christlike to be free from the littlenesses and meannesses that bulge and distort the soul.

"Hewed them cisterns"—that is, hewed for themselves cisterns. Water is indispensable to life. This pictures the demand of the soul. The immortal nature has a thirst which only the living water can satisfy. Seeking to satisfy the soul with other things is what God calls "hewing to themselves cisterns." "Hewing to themselves." Here is the basis of unrest among men, their supreme selfishness; all aims, impulses, thoughts, and efforts toward self.

The larger per cent of mankind are for themselves. They may be in corporations, trusts, or gangs; but they are alone in motive. The maniac multitude in the Stock Exchange in Wall Street are in a throng together, but each is severely to himself and for himself, and Wall Street is the human race in miniature.

Happiness and wretchedness are opposites; the one

introversive, the other extroversive. What the world calls success is introversive, the inflow of every tide upon one's self and developing the earth and the world tendencies of the soul, while the higher and nobler powers shrink and perish. But success in the higher and nobler sense is extroversive. It is the outgoing of the nature toward God and humanity. Who ever loved and did not give out the whole soul? And who ever loved and did not experience a happiness supreme? "It is more blessed to give than to receive." O the blessedness of the giving out of the whole heart!

Every time and season has its lessons and its opportunities. The years past were years of prosperity, years of material success. Men touched the tides and turned them in upon themselves. But a change has come, a stagnant state, a time of stringency and meager circulation; men out of employment who know not whence to-morrow's bread will come, while the awful echoes of unprecedented war come to us from across the seas. What of all this? Is God in this pressure? Was he God in the prosperous period, and is he not God in the stagnant season? Has he no lesson for us now?

Ah! this is God's year, his season of special opportunity. This is the growing time for souls, the time for development of the nobler things in men. The conditions now will open wide the avenues of sympathy and generosity and make men forget themselves for a time. Never was there such want and helplessness in our land—more unemployed to-day than at any time since the landing of the Mayflower on American shores; men and women with burdens too great for their strength, who are dying for a word, a look, a hand grasp of encouragement; men to whom the smallest kindness will be as "the shadow of a great rock in a weary land." Never was there such opportunity for the highest achievements of the soul.

There may be stagnation in business, and men say, "We can make nothing"; but there is a ready market for the higher and nobler things; the best chance for decades to get rich in those deeds and qualities which make millionaires for eternity. Give us the zeal for the higher things now which men have shown in the prosperous periods after the things that perish, and we will make a record that will create a jubilee in heaven. God help us to know the value of the opportunities of a hard season!

Cistern-digging is hard work. It is downward work, away from the light, into the earth and through the rocks. So "the way of the transgressor is hard." His way is downward, away from God and toward destruction. Sin is consuming. It robs men of peace and rest and sleep and brings redness of eyes and distress of countenance. Its dangers are typified in the text.

I knew a well digger who had followed that business until he had become indifferent to danger. He was at work in confident safety, but had not curbed and made safe the walls above him, and in a moment he was buried alive by their falling. Another had taken the precaution to curb the walls; but the slender curbing suddenly gave way, and he perished.

Thus men are confident while carving out a sinful

life. One says, "There is no danger"; another says, "I have fortified at the danger points"; but both alike perish. There is no moment of safety to the man living in sin. You cannot so curb the walls of sin that they may not fall in upon you. The outraged laws of nature and of God hang over the sinner and may crush him at any moment. How often life caves in upon men, crushed in a moment by their own neglect and sins! So with many in the Church who have gaps and chasms in their Christian life. "Not right with God just now, but planning to do better after a certain time."

We had a noble-hearted friend who made the race for a lucrative office. He felt that to succeed he must use measures out of harmony with his character as a Christian man. We urged him not to take such a course; but he persisted and made the race. Worn by the work of the canvass, he went to the springs for a short time and wrote me that he would take up his Church work as soon as he got home and live right. He was brought home in his coffin. Life caved in upon him.

"Broken cisterns, that can hold no water." The Orientals often dug and filled and then concealed their cisterns and left them for times of drought. Sometimes the walls or bottom would crack and the water escape. Then when they came to use the water in the season of drought, in place of refreshing water they found only the settlings and offensive mud at the bottom.

What a picture of the deceptive and ruinous nature of a sinful or worldly life—to give life's vigor to worldly affairs, forgetting God and giving all the powers to time and sense, expecting happiness and satisfaction from these things in the evening time of life, and then to reap the results! In the soul's thirst in life's afternoon men look for rest in the things in which they have invested life. How fearful it is when they find it only a broken cistern! No refreshment, but only disappointment and disgust! O the regrets of a wasted life! The mud in the cistern's base! The loathsome leavings of a misspent probation!

I have seen the man with broken spirit when the world had failed on his hands, the devotee of dissipation when nature's forces were exhausted, the woman of the world when youth and conquest were no longer hers. Wasted lives! Broken cisterns!

They forsook the fountain of living waters. The contrast between the flowing fountain and the broken cistern pictures the contrast between God and the world. Men draw and drink from pleasure's wells, but they drink at a cost. The night of revelry is at the cost of unrest and exhaustion. Dissipation costs thirst, compunction, and mental disquiet. Men pay largely for the world's brackish and ofttimes poisonous draughts. To be carnally-minded is death. But spiritual pleasures are fountain draughts. The waters are flowing and pure. The more placid and quiet the soul and body, the richer and sweeter the joys. The deepest draughts are in the calm and holy stillness of the soul. There can be no intemperance here. We cannot drink to excess. There are mineral springs whose waters are so light and soft that you may constantly drink with impunity. This faintly portrays that living water of which we may drink perpetually:

> "Insatiate to this spring I fly;
> I drink and yet am ever dry."

The Overflow and Everflow.

What is this world and life and all that is beautiful? What but the overflow of this fountain, the overflow of God, the overflow of his thought, his power, his beneficence, his love? O, if we could but realize that the joys of home, the sweets of friendship, the grandeurs of imagination, the luxury of love, and all that makes up the riches of being are but streams from this fountain! God is behind it all.

We have never yet conceived of what a God we have. He is a better God, a richer God, a more loving and compassionate God than we have ever thought. How sacred every joy when we realize it as direct from him! How deathless are spiritual joys! Near my childhood home was a great, pure, flowing spring. The red man doubtless drank from it a thousand years ago. I drank from it in my boyhood, and others perhaps will drink from it a thousand years to come. Where does it come from, and why does it last? Because it is a fountain and has its supply deep down amid the rock ribs of the mountains. When lake and well and pool and cistern are dry and forgotten, it will flow on, simply because it is a fountain. The source and resources of the world's pleasures will one day cease and dry up forever, but the immortal soul will live on. Its hunger and thirst will still call for gratification, its demands as deathless as its nature. Then let us draw ever nearer and never turn from the Living Fountain, where we may partake of that water of which if a man drink he shall never thirst.

WHAT TO DO FIRST.

Text: "But seek ye first the kingdom of God." (Matt. vi. 33.)

HAPPY is the man when much is to be done who knows what to do first! When the soul comes to conscious accountability and stands upon the threshold of its own unmade destiny looking into the future, Divine Wisdom speaks, telling that soul what to do first: "Seek the kingdom of God."

Do this in order to have room. The first essential to a grand work is plenty of room. Let other possibilities be what they may, you can do but little when you lack room. You cannot do a wholesale business in a six-foot space. Having resources to build broadly, you must have ample grounds for the purpose. When God determined to situate the vast family of man, he prepared ample room; he "created the heavens and the earth"; he did not make such a structure as would circumscribe and cramp the race in future and lead him to see that he had built upon too small a scale.

The soul's first need is room, and this it has not in its natural state. About as narrow a thing as can be found is an unregenerate heart. It is a small affair and only large enough for its own selfish interests and those of its family and special friends. The intellect may be broad, and there may be good impulses; but there is no room for God. The heart's inn is full, and Christ goes, as his mother went to give him birth, to a place of less dignity.

The kingdom of God has infinite room, and the soul that finds it finds room for time and eternity. How it expands the soul when it finds this kingdom! The man may have been a diminutive, narrow, contracted creature in his moral nature, but when he is converted he has room enough to admit all humanity. He loves everybody and loves God with a love that is boundless and full of joy. Everything in range of a man gets larger when he gets fairly into the kingdom of God.

The Crowded Man.

There are men who seem always to be crowded and oppressed. They are not well out into the kingdom. They may be just inside, but are against the wall. One hasn't much room when he is against the wall; he feels that there is not room enough for any other man's opinions that do not agree with his. The Church is too small for him and some others who decline to do just what he dictates. Even the neighborhood gets too small for him and his neighbors for both to be comfortable. Sometimes there is not room enough in the family for him and the other members to live in harmony. But when he gets fairly out into the kingdom of God, how everything expands! The home, the Church, the neighborhood all get large enough then. What a sense of relief it is to get away out into the kingdom, where we are neither crowded nor smothered; out where everybody is not against us, rasping, annoying, and striving to take advantage of us!

Here we have a place to put things. You cannot put large, first-class furniture in a little coop of a parlor. Undertake it, and you will find when it is done that you have no room to turn around and are compelled to back out. You would then give almost anything for the only thing you cannot get, and that is room.

There is not room for a fine and finished character, with a first-class set of graces, outside the kingdom of God. The unregenerate may have fine traits, but the set of soul furniture is not complete. How often we hear it said, "All that man lacks is religion"! But he lacks that; he lacks room. If he would only come into the kingdom, what a grand and useful man he would be! The fruits of the spirit are love, joy, peace, gentleness, meekness, temperance, faith. These find room for protection only in the kingdom of God. There alone can they live and flourish.

The Expanding Life.

The beginner in business who is without capital wants only a stand on the street corner or at most a few feet front with a one-story building, but when capital accrues he shifts from the small lot and the little one story to broader ground and a more commodious building on the two- or three-story style.

A life outside the kingdom of God is a one-story affair. Honest and morally correct it may be, but it cannot be broad while God has not a place in it. The grand life is the two-story life, the life that adds on the divine to the human, the life that takes God in. The life that pulls down the old fabric lays a broader foundation and builds on a grander scale; rebuilds the old morality, the ground story, with an open glass front, then builds the second story, God's department, with a supernatural symmetry and a skylight looking heavenward and bringing the divine sunlight down into every department of his being. How magnificent the life that is broad and high and open toward God and flooded with the sunshine of his abiding presence!

Remodel a single building in a block, and it gives a touch of beauty to the buildings round about it. A remodeled life is grander than a remodeled and beautified building. When one man or half a dozen men whose lives have been dilapidated and mildewed by sin come into the kingdom and are converted to God and begin to walk in the beauty of holiness, it lifts the whole community to a higher plane and stirs a breeze among the angels. "There is joy in heaven over one sinner that repenteth." Heaven has joy in every remodeled life.

Never Too Much Room.

There is much vacancy in the things of this life— an emptiness that is painful, a great farm with only here and there a spot in cultivation, a huge house with scant furnishings, a great church with a scattered few within it like mourners about a tomb. How hollow and hungry these things appear! Did you ever see a parlor that looked lean and hungry for another piece of furniture? a Church which had fed on half-meal audiences until it looked lean and thin? Thus we miss it many times in measurement. But there is no such emptiness in the kingdom of God. However great the space we appropriate, there is wealth to fill it. Disproportion, hollowness, and hunger are not in kings' houses. The leanness and poverty of the soul are with the children of this world and not with the children of the kingdom. There need be no hollow and half-filled lives among the children of God. Though the home be a cottage, and that the humblest, yet if the child of God be there it is a king in a cottage and a life as full and beautiful as though in the palace royal.

Room for Perpetual Filling.

Things under the sun get grown and can become no larger, get full and can hold no more. The physical reaches a maturity it cannot pass. The oak attains a height beyond which it cannot go. Military men reach the height of their glory, orators get grown, preachers get grown, nations reach a renown that they cannot pass; but in the kingdom of God, in the supernatural, there are no fixed bounds. The cruel and crushing lines of limit have never been laid in that realm.

The rich man had to pull down his old barns and build new ones to store his goods. There is no such necessity there. However great the income of heavenly riches, there will be no lack of room. Here in this life the soul may add grace to grace and beauty to beauty until it ascends out of the mortal and then add glory to glory with that perpetual compound income that will follow the joint heir with Christ. Paul is not yet oppressed by his weight of glory. The man who comes into the kingdom of God finds the place to begin and complete his destiny—a roomy place, a place for a large life, a full life, an everlasting life. "Seek ye first the kingdom of God."

The Greater and the Lesser Lights.

Text: "And God made two great lights; the greater light to rule the day, and the lesser light to rule the night." (Gen. i. 16.)

CREATION and redemption are the elder and the younger sons of the Divine Energy, the Judah and Benjamin of the Infinite. Creation is the child of his power; redemption is the child of his love; and the elder shall serve the younger. Creation shall serve until the redemption work is complete. All things are yours. The record of creation is the first edition of the gospel. Dry as these old writings seem, they are full of gospel oil. Like the pine knot that needs only the touch of the spark, these chronicles flame under the touch of the Holy Ghost. Horeb rocks they are which gush with living water at his touch; sun and moon, representatives of Christ and his Church.

Great Lights.

In magnitude they are above all others, yet in such disproportion that one is called the greater and the other the lesser light. These are the chief agents for the diffusion of light. Blot them out, and original darkness will settle back upon the face of the deep. Christ and the Church are the greater and lesser lights in the moral universe. He is the Light that lighteth every man that cometh into the world, and he says of the Church: "Ye are the light of the world." Take these away, and humanity will have a sunless day and moonless night.

As the smaller lights gather radiance from the sun, so the minor agencies, helpful to humanity, have their resources in Christ. After all that science has done, if Christ and the Church be taken from the world, moral darkness will become its perpetual shroud.

They were made for this earth. Whatever influence the sun may have on other worlds and other systems, he was made for one special purpose—to give light upon the earth, to be a perpetual minister to us. Whether there be other and fallen worlds, and whether the crimson lines of redemption have gone out to them, we may not say; but one thing we know, God loved this world. The Saviour, like the sun, was sent especially to this world. He was conceived and born into this world, baptized here, crucified and buried here. He died for our sins according to the Scriptures.

"And God set them in the firmament of the heaven." The earth has never known a still hour. Its very existence is motion. There has been no pause in its ceaseless whirling. The seasons have chased the seasons through the circles and cycles; generation has succeeded generation as the sand grains drop from the hourglass of time. But the sun has held his place.

We look on him to-day, the same that shot his virgin beams down through Eden's glassy pools, the same that Adam saw, the same that lighted Abraham's tent and shone on Joshua's battling hosts, the same that lights the world to-day.

While we do not see the faces of all our friends, yet we walk in the same light and see the same sun, and thus are we one in heaven's broad sunshine.

Jesus Christ is lifted up and set in the moral mid-heaven and is drawing all men unto him. Changes continue — astronomical, geological, geographical. Humanity rolls on as a tide. The generations chase each other as the billows of the sea; but Christ remains the same yesterday, to-day, and forever. And though we be not face to face with our fellow soldiers, yet we dwell in the same light and see the same Christ.

The Influence of the Sun.

Here is a wealth of thought that no pulpit hour nor pulpit power can portray. Nature lives from the sun. All things may look to him and say: "All my springs are in thee."

> "Center of light and energy, thy way
>   Is through the unknown void; thou hast thy throne,
> Morning and evening, and at the close of day
>   Far in the blue, untended and alone."

He shines that all nature may have life and have it more abundantly. His resurrection power is going forth at this present springtime. At his touch the dead are rising. The violet and the crocus are having part in the first resurrection. The whole kingdom feels his power, from the spear grass and the lichen to the magnolia and the oak. Soon will beauty burst from bud and bulb with grace of waving bough and billowy grain and music of insect life and warbling tribes, all due to the midheaven sun. Here is the annual picture. Humanity owes its beauty to Christ. Crimson in history, corrupt in nature, yet when dominated by him there is moral beauty. All holy heroism, noble self-sacrifice, and beautiful unselfishness are due to Him who is the Light of men. No dell is so dark that the sun cannot fill it with light and no heart so corrupt and hopeless that Christ cannot give it purity and peace.

The Relation of the Sun and the Moon.

The moon is an opaque body, without light or power to give light. Its light is a reflection from the sun. If the earth intervenes between them, it is thrown into eclipse; its glory departs, and it becomes repulsive in its blackness and ruin.

Here we see the Church in her relation to Christ. The Church of itself is morally opaque. However great her numbers, wise her economy, brilliant her paraphernalia, or pompous her service, she is lifeless and lightless without Christ. There must be a divine impartation and supernatural domination by Christ himself. Otherwise the Church is a rayless moon, an organization in ruins. Let the world or its ways come between Christ and his Church, and her glory departs. The period known as the Dark Ages was but the Church in eclipse. It is a dark age with that Church or that soul which has passed out of the light of Christ.

Seen Through the Telescope.

The moon is a vast ruin. Why has God used a globe in ruins to make a light giver to the world? The rayless moon, desolate and dark, is the background for the glory of the sun. The moonbeams are but the softened and second-hand sunshine flung back upon us at stilly night, as hour after hour that passionless face climbs the desolate blue.

The Church is made from humanity in ruins. Moonlike, she has of herself no vestige of life or beauty. Of all dead things, a dead Church is the deadest. Amid mausoleums, catacombs, cemeteries, and sepulchers there are no dead like a dead Church. Zion at her best estate is only imperfection mantled in the divine glory—"the beauty of the Lord our God upon her."

Shadows.

Though the moon be covered by the glory of the sun, her wild fastnesses and repulsive ruin veiled, still there are shadows upon her disk. Zion, with her transgressions forgiven and her sins covered, yet has shadows upon her face. A stain here, a blot there, a bit of cloud yonder, still she gives light. She is the Church of God, after all. Some might criticize and discard the moon because of its shadows, but God does not. Neither will he discard nor forsake his Church because she is not perfect. Like the moon marching through midheaven, the shadows upon her face but giving light in the nighttime, God's Church holds her place and flings her light into the moral midnight of this fallen world, showing men the path of life and riding on in her majesty and power, regardless of the shadows that have fallen upon her in her march.

The Light Source Invisible.

When the moon gives light by night, the sun is hidden from our view, invisible to us, but in full view of the moon. In her exalted place she is face to face with the fountain of her light, far enough from the earth to see the sun. Whereas if she were nearer the earth she could neither have light nor benefit the earth. The moon can light the earth only by keeping above it and far enough from it to catch the light of the sun.

Can anything be more grandly symbolic of the office and work of the Church? Zion must take high ground. She must stand above and separate from the world, where she may move in an orbit of absolute purity. She can bless the world only by keeping above it and far enough from it. The compromise spirit, falling into the world's way in order to save the world, is a fatal mistake. It is but the moon coming down upon the bosom of the earth in order to give it benefit. Bring the moon too close, and her light expires and she becomes worthless and repulsive. Let the Church come into fellowship with the world, and her glory departs, while the world laughs and mocks at her helplessness.

Magnitude of the Moon.

It is forty-nine times less than the earth, yet it is called a great light; not a great body, but a great light. Take away the starry hosts, and the moon gives more light than they all. Small as a body without resources, yet drawing supplies from the sun, she lights a globe forty-nine times larger than herself.

Here we have the Church as proportioned to the world. In magnitude the Church compares with the world as the moon with the earth, as one to forty-nine; but as a light giver the Church is only second to Christ himself. Eliminate the other lights—science, the brotherhoods, the orders, and others akin—and the Church gives more light than they all. Though the world be forty-nine times larger, yet if the Church do but keep in her high and pure orbit she will light the world unto the perfect day. Who can tell the power of one man of God in a city or community?

Influence of the Moon upon the Earth.

Earth and ocean feel its strange but silent power. The tides ebb and flow by its force. The mighty lungs of the ocean contract and expand by the power of the moon. Earth yields to this power and germinates or rots the seed, matures or blasts the harvests under this lunar influence. Thus the Church affects the world. Christianity wields a strange power over men. They hear the gospel; and while they may not yield, yet the impression abides in their life and character. The Church lays the hand of her silent power upon the great sea of humanity and controls its moral tides, lights in the moral heavens to give light upon the earth.

Our Own Responsibility.

This is in proportion to our position. Yonder forest oak is responsible for the fruit it can produce and the shade it can fling to its utmost length. The sun in midheaven is responsible as far as his rays can reach. O sun and moon, earth is committed to thy care, thine own dependent and helpless charge! How faithful thou art to the trust! The sun says: "I will give thee light and life; I will cause the tribes to grow and the face to shine with gladness." The moon declares: "I will guard thee in the nighttime and rock and lull thee with the changing tides and, like the faithful nurse, will watch thee in the silence as thou sleepest under my soft and subdued light." "Ye are the light of the world." Shall we care for the souls of men as the lights in the firmament care for their charge?

There is now a resurrection nigh. A million seeds and bulbs begin to feel the thrill. Some are coming forth, and soon all nature will be risen from the dead. Shall dead humanity not feel the power God has vested in us? Shall new hope, new love, new life spring up in any soul because of our influence with him who is the resurrection and the life? May God teach us from the skies and give to us this divine, this helpful, this resurrection power!

Peter's Fall.

Text: "And Peter followed him afar off, even into the palace of the high priest: and he sat with the servants, and warmed himself at the fire." (Mark xiv. 54.)

THAT we may fall from a gracious state is not only taught in the Scriptures, but it is sadly illustrated in all ages and in all Churches. This is a fact, and there is no argument against a fact. Peter's is a sad case, and we will note the slippery steps that others may see and shun his shame.

The Conditions Favorable to Falling.

There are times when the danger is greater than at others. Peter's fall occurred at one of the times of danger. Before the Master's arrest and while he was working miracles and the multitudes were wanting to crown him king, Peter was not in much danger. It was an easy thing for him to come to the front. He loved to be in front and meant what he said when he declared himself ready to go with the Master to prison or unto death. But the scene changed. Christ became a prisoner. Then Peter's courage cooled, and he began to seek shelter from the storm.

Thus it is with us. When the Church is revived and the multitudes are strewing palm branches and shouting hosannas, it is no hard matter for us at such times to come to the front. It is a sorry disciple who cannot stand for Christ in time of revival. How bold we become! We feel then that we could go with him to prison or to death. But when the revival has passed, there are many that get too timid to venture near the church oftener than once a month. The danger is after the revival, when the devil rallies his forces and seeks to retake the ground he has lost. Now let us note the steps in Peter's fall.

The First Step.

"He followed him afar off." He allowed himself to get too far from Christ. This is the first step to ruin. Had he kept near the Master, his faith would not have failed him. But he hung back and thought to follow him at a distance. That afar-off territory is dangerous territory. He was afraid; and the farther he fell back, the deeper his fear became. The Master had told him to put up his sword, and I doubt not that he threw it away, as I am sure he did not have it buckled about him as he sat with the servants. Peter had a terrible night of it, unarmed and scared half to death, creeping with the tread of a cat through the darkness, startled at every sound, and even alarmed at the fluttering of his own heart. He loved his Master and could not give him up, yet he was afraid to face his foes and stand by him in the hour of peril.

Here is the first degree, the entered apprentice de-degree, in apostasy. There are those who really love Christ, but are afraid to let it be known, and hence they try to follow him on the sly. And following afar off, they are afraid—afraid to talk with a sinner about his soul, lest he get mad; afraid to go to a prayer meeting, lest they be called on to lead the prayer; afraid to pray in secret, because some one might see them on their knees before the Lord; and, therefore, like Peter, they are unarmed and unprepared to do battle for Christ.

But you say: "I do not want to seem forward or officious." I felt just that way when I was in the army. If there ever was a time when I did not want to seem forward, it was just as we were going into battle. But the only cure for fear is to get close and keep close to Christ. Let the cry of the soul be: "Nearer, my God, to thee; nearer to thee."

Second Step.

He sat with the servants, took his place among the enemies of Christ. The one who is found afar off will soon be found with the enemy. And Christ's enemies were never more numerous at Jerusalem than they now are in our land. It was a motley mob that surrounded him, but it was representative. You can detect them now, just as they detected Peter. They said: "Thy speech betrayeth thee." You can tell them by their speech. The man who argues for the world and its follies, whose words are irreverent and profane, and whose lips are foul; the woman whose heart is fixed upon the world, whose god is style, and who laughs when religion is derided—these are Christ's enemies, no matter what their social position; whether they be the sons and daughters of the high priest or the obscure servants about the kitchen fire, they are his enemies.

Let a Christian keep such company, associate for a time with the servants of sin, then ask him about his religion, and he will tell you: "I don't profess to know much of Christ and never claimed to be very religious." Peter loved his Master even when sitting with his enemies, but he was too weak to confess it. Many a poor soul really loves Christ, but, without courage, is hanging between him and the world and is about as happy as Peter was on that memorable night.

Peter among the Roman servants excites our sympathy. The Christian among Christ's enemies is always to be pitied. I care not at what time or place, your association with the world, like that of Peter, is followed by bitterness and weeping. A wholehearted, uncompromising consecration that never sits down with the servants of sin is the safeguard against those seasons of shame and remorse.

Third Step.

"He warmed himself by their fire," put himself under obligation to them. Woe to the man who compromises his relation to Christ to gain the favor of the world! Do this, and your hands are tied and your tongue silenced. We cannot well accept the world's favors and then rise up and rebuke its sins. This has been one of the curses of the Church, warming herself at the world's fires, taking leprous wealth into her membership, giving impurity prominence in her official posts, her ministers condoning corruption. A man with a million, made by oppressing or even debauching and destroying his fellows, his hands made too slippery with innocent blood to hold, covers that hand with a kid glove, and the minister takes it and gives him welcome into the Church. I have known a Christian college built by the Church and owned by the Church deny its relation to the Church simply to get the benefit of the money of a godless millionaire.

The world has good fires. It has plenty of material out of which to build them and is glad enough when the Church will consent to sit and warm herself by them. I know the Church is often very thinly clad and shivering for want of the world's comforts; but, like her great Founder, who was poorer than the foxes and the birds, she had better not have where to lay her head than be wrapped in the devil's down and sitting at the feet of the world.

Peter was doubtless very cold, and the Roman fire was very tempting; but it would have been better for him to have kept his blood warm during that night in some other way; better for him had he run races with himself all night or sat down and shivered it out, even if he had been frostbitten. I had rather be frostbitten than disgraced. "Better to enter into life having one foot or one eye, rather than having two eyes or two feet and be cast into hell."

Fourth and Final Step.

He swore that he did not know the Master. Here is the climax in his downward course. If you can admit a climax downward, here it is. He gets too far from Christ, goes over to the enemies, puts himself under obligation to them, then swears that he doesn't know the Lord. This is awful, but just as natural as it is awful. There are thousands who were once converted, then grew cold at heart, then identified themselves with the godless, then gave up their faith, and are now blasphemers and haters of Christ. It is an awful fact that souls do fall from a gracious state. Earth and hell have hopeless examples of this dreadful truth. Therefore, "Let him that thinketh he standeth take heed lest he fall." Keep close to the Master, and when among the wicked be humble but bold. Speak out with the true Galilean ring. If you warm at the world's fires, do it, as the Master ate with publicans and sinners, without compromise. Let them know they are befriending Christ when they befriend you. Above all, be courageous. "Be strong in the Lord, and in the power of his might."

Danger is not from weakness. The only danger to the child of God is in sin, not in weakness. See that tiny vine just beginning to climb that giant oak. What is weaker than that little vine? What could it do in a storm? What would it be under the tread of a beast? But it is clinging to the oak, and every day it gets stronger and creeps up higher and puts forth new tendrils and twines about the grand oak. Thus it rises higher and higher and never allows itself to be loosened from the tree, until after a time it reaches as high as the oak itself.

Here is what weakness can do by simply clinging to strength. Christ is our strength, mightier to the weakest saint than the giant oak to the tiny vine. Only cling to Christ and find some new beauty in his character each day around which you may twine a love tendril and thus make your union with him closer and ever closer until in perfect Christlikeness you shall come to full heirship and ultimately to eternal rulership with him.

THE CONQUEST OF IMPENITENCE.

Text: "And one of the malefactors which were hanged railed on him, saying, If thou be Christ, save thyself and us." (Luke xxiii. 39.)

THESE bitter words are all that is recorded of this man. They begin with an "if" and indicate his infidel life and hopeless death—like one of later history who said when dying: "O God, if there be a God, have mercy on my soul, if I have a soul."

Men exhaust the gospel forces. The obstinacy of the human will is equal to this, and this malefactor illustrates this awful truth. All forces are subservient to the gospel. Hence every force may become a gospel force. Even the wrath of man is made to praise God.

Love is the first and chief gospel power. Here we see it in its sublimest form. Suffering, bleeding, seeing the wagging heads and hearing the mockings of the rabble, Christ prays: "Father, forgive them, for they know not what they do." Here is love in agony and ignominy, yet praying for and finding apology for its persecutors. This malefactor witnessed divine love in its highest expression and did not repent. That which changed his companion in sin failed to affect him. The same love that failed on him has failed on others in all ages. Every soul that remains impenitent does so against all the force of divine love. God has tried it in every form on the sinners who hear him now—in the quiet form of daily blessings, in health and good fortune, in heart ties and sweet association. He has put it in prayer and song and sermon. He has lifted it before you in agony, groans, and blood; and yet, like this dying malefactor, you have resisted its power.

Physical elements yield to the forces. Niagara's current undermined her stony base, and Table Rock tumbled into the mighty tide. The touch of time tells upon the everlasting hills, and the wear of the centuries affects every material element; but the mightiest gospel forces play upon the impenitent heart without effect.

> "The rocks can rend, the earth can quake,
> The seas can roar, the mountains shake;
> Of feeling all things show some sign,
> But this unfeeling heart of mine."

Convulsed nature did not affect him. Nothing strikes men with awe and alarm so quickly as a strange phenomenon in nature. Let nature get out of harness, and the world is impressed. When the stars fell in the early part of the century, there was great alarm and crying to God. In the Charleston earthquake there was much praying in the streets, and men left off swearing for days afterwards.

God uses earthquakes to bring men to repentance. The Philippian jailer was converted through the moral power of an earthquake. His was a genuine conversion; hence it will not to do say that earthquake repentance is not genuine. But this poor wretch was unmoved by the convulsion of nature. The quaking earth, the darkened heavens, and the rending rocks—enough to strike terror to the heart of the hardest—have no effect upon him. His obstinacy was equal to all the force of a convulsed universe. He could hang above a world that did shake and tremble with feeling and still curse his God. Such is the hardness of impenitence. God may speak through storm, cyclone, earthquake, or flood; but the impenitent heart is indifferent to the alarms. Every impenitent has felt such forces and resisted them.

The change in others did not affect him. The moral power of Christ's death changed his persecutors into penitents. The multitude that wagged their heads and mocked returned smiting their breasts.

Christ had more believers before he was dead an hour than in all his ministry. It is not simply the Christ, but the crucified Christ, that causes men's hearts to break. Right where his heart broke with dying love is the point from which issues the only power that can break the hearts of sinful men. "I, if I be lifted up, will draw all men unto me." O the magnetism of that cross! A world of dying men can feel it, and the preaching of to-day has power in precise proportion to its proximity to that cross.

But although even the rabble were convinced, this dying wretch was unmoved. Here is a feature of inveterate impenitence. The gospel that convicts and saves the publicans and harlots fails to save many who rank in society and live under the shadow of the church. You see dissipated men, corrupt men, bloody men changed and transformed by the power of the gospel; while you, like this malefactor, remain impenitent. Have you not seen the worst of men changed by this power? And what influence has it had upon you?

Death does not produce repentance. Here is this multitude moved and convicted by the strange divine power that issued from the dead Nazarene while yet on the cross. This convicted multitude is in no danger of death, while this unfortunate man hangs over the very abyss of death and yet is moved only to accusation and railing. Away with the idea that it will be easy to repent when we come in sight of death! This man is now in sight of it, but he utters curses in place of prayers. Death will bring despair, but not repentance. The cry then will be for the rocks and mountains to fall upon and hide them from the wrath of the Lamb.

The example of his comrade was powerless. His fellow thief had a genuine conversion. We know it, because he began at once to rebuke and exhort his companion: "Dost thou not fear God?" Here is an infallible sign of genuine conversion, when the convert seeks to get others saved. That was my first thought when converted, and it was doubtless yours. I must and did go to seek my companions to get them saved. The last words of this new convert on the cross are words of warning. Born of God, he begins at once to preach to his companion in sin; but his change and his words are without effect upon his impenitent fellow convict.

Impenitent friend, hear us now! You have seen multitudes saved, and, like this man, you have seen your own companions changed. Those who were once with you in sin are not with you now. They left you and turned to God. You have seen the change in them, and many perhaps are the warnings they have given you; but, like the impenitent on the cross, you have resisted their example and their warnings. You have seen enough in the change of your old companions to have led you to Christ.

You may object to the preacher and say: "He does not know my peculiar temperament and disposition. He does not know how to sympathize with me. He preaches to me because that is his profession. He warns me as a part of the work he is paid to do. He exhorts me just as he would plow or hoe in his cornfield." But this man on the cross is hearing the gospel from his fellow in crime. He knows he is in earnest. He knows it is no paid performance with him. Have you not been exhorted by your converted comrades, those whom you knew to be sincere and in sympathy with you and doing what they did for your good alone? And, marvelous to tell, you are impenitent yet.

His own punishment was powerless. All else failing, surely his suffering will cause him to relent. The torn nerves, the lacerated flesh, the mangled feet and hands, the unutterable agony from suspension on the dreadful spikes—surely under all this he will break down and cry for mercy. But not so. His utterances are railings upon the innocent Nazarene that suffers by his side, mingled with taunts of unbelief: "If thou be Christ, save thyself and us."

Even intense suffering may not work moral reform. All the force of suffering is here brought to bear. His suffering could hardly be intensified, and still he utters doubts and rails in madness as he hangs over despair. He is between Christ and hell. Both are near at hand. He is equally close to each, and yet he dies cursing. His conscious nearness to death does not change him.

Will conquers all. How many grow worse under the agonies of an impenitent life! Men feel the heavy hand of divine judgments. Things to which they have given thought and heart and effort have proved only nails to tear their hands. Their feet are pierced with spikes which fasten them to crosses from which they can never be free. Thorns pierce not their heads, but their hearts, while remorse with its triple sting can never be removed. Like this unfortunate sufferer, the impenitent is doomed to suffer until life is extinct, and yet the unrest of past years and that of years to come does not bring repentance.

I speak now to men who are exhausting the gospel forces. Dear reader, stop and ask, "Is it I?" Men who are measuring arms with God's forbearance, proving yourselves more than a match for divine mercy, you can overcome all the saving influences and agencies; you can subdue the angel of mercy and send him away grieved and to return no more. Thousands have proved themselves a match for this angel. But there is another you cannot overcome. This dying representative of yours could not overcome the death angel. You may never surrender to mercy, but you will surrender to death.

How many gospel forces have you overcome? Have you vanquished the power of divine love? Have the mighty movements of nature had no effect? Have the multitudes you have seen saved had no effect whatever? Has the repenting of your associates failed to touch your hardened nature? Have the heart agonies of your whole life been without effect? Then behold your prototype. He conquered all. And you are nigh the hour of ultimate triumph. The hour is nigh when, like him, you will make good your own awful and eternal doom. The saving influences are all now behind you. He had but to wait until the decline of the evening, and they came and broke his bones and ended the drama. Death, like the Parthian soldiers, is now on his way; and you have but to wait a little time, and the breaking bones will end the scene.

Autobiography of Bishop Henry Clay Morrison.

May the Holy Spirit help you to repent as you read these lines and change your thought from the doubting "If thou be Christ" to the cry of the saved sufferer, "Lord, remember me when thou comest into thy kingdom"!

Union with Christ.

Text: "I am the vine, ye are the branches." (John xv. 5.)

THIS union with Christ is so real and vital that the Christ life pervades our life, our burdens become his burdens, our sorrows his sorrows,, and our heartbeat his heartbeat.

How We Obtain This Branchhood.

We are by nature branches of another vine and unallied to Christ, a nature averse to him and desperately allied to sin; hence if we become branches of the true Vine there must be a process of grafting. In this process the twig must first be severed from the parent stock and skillfully connected with the new ,stock, insomuch that the new life becomes its life; and henceforth it lives not unto itself, but unto the new body.

Thus do we become members of the true Vine. The work begins with a separation from the old life. The keen steel of repentance must sever the soul from its old idols and sins. The surgery of salvation in all its dreadfulness comes in at this point and begins the work of cutting off right hands and plucking out right eyes. There is a hospital experience, a sin sickness, and here we come in touch with the Great Physician.

There must be heart-bleeding which separates us from the old-nature life. Herein is the basis of weakness in the Church and in many Christian lives. It is the effort to evade this soul surgery and this hospital experience. Too many have never been separated from the old-nature life nor felt the keen edge of the divine instrument severing them from their old sins. Changing the figure, it is the thrusting in of the plowshare of repentance that subsoils the soul and tears out the roots of bitterness and prepares for splendid growth. The strength of the after life with the Christain is in proportion to the depth and genuineness of his repentance. The deepest soul sickness precedes the most robust health and growth.

The Nature of This Relation.

The grafting does not change the individuality. Graft the apple twig on the pear stock, and it still produces apples. Graft the cherry on the peach, and it still produces cherries. It holds its individuality and draws its new life from the new stock. This is the law in the spiritual realm. Conversion neither changes nor destroys the individuality. Human individuality is changeless; it is God's stamp upon the immortal nature, which neither time nor eternity can change. The man is the same in form, feature, and intellect after conversion that he was before it. If you knew him before, you will recognize him afterwards. The only difference is that he is filled with a new life. He is the same in his individuality, whether that be peach, pippin, or crab. He is filled with that new life which makes him larger and richer and nobler in his spiritual nature.

Religion does not disrupt nor change that beautiful variety which God has established in the intellectual and social world. Like the parent stock that nourishes all varieties grafted into it, the true vine gives abundant life to all classes of humanity. Whatever nature may have done or not done for a man will not affect his possibilities in grace. If he will quit sin and come to Christ, all possibilities are his. Our religion is not intended to remodel our organism, but our life and character; to fill us with those divine elements which produce the fruits of the spirit—love, joy, peace, gentleness, and all the divine cluster.

All the varieties in the universe can grow in the Church—little souls and big souls, peculiar people and odd people, narrow minds and broad minds, sweet spirits and sour spirits, the royal blushing pippin and the little rusty crab—but all draw life and grow and ripen by this union with Christ, the true Vine.

The Design of This Relation.

God runs the universe with one single aim, and that is production. He turns the world over every day and rolls it around the sun every year and marshals the seasons and draws upon the sea and gathers the clouds and sends the rains. There are budding and blooming and fading and falling, and all with an eye to fruit. What a process it is! Leaves, flowers, blades are small things to him. It is fruit he demands, the full corn in the ear.

God's one design with us is fruitfulness in Christian life. "Herein is my Father glorified, that ye bear much fruit." Not how much summer time nor how much bloom and sweetness nor how much emotional joy, but how much fruit. This requirement is strictly personal. I may complain that the Church doesn't flourish. He doesn't require the Church to flourish; he requires that you and I shall flourish.

I love the fervors of religion. I love to see and scent the blooms and hear the hum of bees, but I had rather enjoy the ripe and luscious grapes than see and hear all these. So it is fruit that God wants. Fruit alone will meet the demand.

The Pruning Is to This End.

This process is severely singular. Notice this word "every." It is repeated: every branch that beareth fruit and every branch that beareth not fruit. The vinedresser does not prune his vines as the harvester mows his grain, cutting a thousand stalks at a stroke; but, knife in hand, he takes hold of branch by branch and cuts and prunes as each may require.

"Every branch that beareth not fruit he taketh away." Here is the lopping off and the reason for it; not because the branch is small or near the ground or only able to bear a little fruit, but because it is absolutely fruitless.

God will not cut me off because I am the least or lowest branch on the vine; nor will he cut me off because I have no special gifts that the world admires. It is not attractiveness but fruitfulness that he demands. Neither will he destroy me because I can produce only a little fruit. "The bruised reed will he not break, and the smoking flax will he not quench." The blessed Vine supports and nourishes a multitude of poor, little, almost worthless branches, but he is even more tender with them than with the stronger ones. We have but one thing to fear—that is fruitlessness—but we may well fear this as we would the fire that is not quenched. The fruitless branch is soon cut off, and the cut-off branch is soon in the flames.

Every One to Feel the Pruning Knife.

The fruitless branch is cut off and the fruitful branch pruned. The fruitless soul is destroyed and the fruitful soul pruned that it may bring forth more fruit. His disciples illustrated this law. Judas was cut off, and the others were made to bleed and suffer while they maintained their allegiance to Christ. Trials are no proof of God's displeasure, but an evidence of our true discipleship. Note the one hundred and forty and four thousand before the throne who went up through great tribulation.

Your little child is never dearer than when under correction. It looks up through its tears to beg for pardon. God's child is never dearer to him than when it looks up through its tears, which come from the pruning touch, and says: "Father, not mine, but thy will be done." God was never closer to Job than when he sat on the ash heap, never closer to Daniel than when he slept in the den, and the only time he was ever visible to the Hebrew brothers was when they walked through the fiery furnace. Then let us learn to see his hand in the dark things of life. Faith sees

Autobiography of Bishop Henry Clay Morrison.

him as well in the darkness as in the light. The clouds are his chariots.

More fruit is God's demand. He prunes the fruitful branches that they may bring forth more fruit. The divine aim is to increase our usefulness. We aim at increase in fields, flocks, merchandise, and income. No man is willing to remain in business at a monotonous standstill. With improved facilities and experience he expects increased success. The same is true in the divine husbandry. God expects not only fruit, but more fruit, and the pruning process is to this end; and yet it is sad work.

See that vine propitiously planted in strong soil and fair to the sun? It has shot out its branches and taken more than ordinary prominence. Covered with luxuriant foliage, it seems of more than ordinary promise. But examine it, and you find it is principally foliage with but little fruit, perhaps a few defective clusters hid away and half rotten under the heavy leaves. It is almost a cumberer of the ground. But the vinedresser comes with the pruning knife and cuts away the pretentious foliage. Branches are lopped off, tendrils cut, and the sappy earth life flows from a hundred wounds. Now it stands a humbled, subdued, and bleeding thing and well-nigh shorn of its earthliness. But the sunshine comes with its ministries. The oozing wounds cauterize and heal, and soon it rallies from the terrible pruning. Then the fruit buds begin to appear; no grand and pretentious offshoots now, but tiny clusters are forming by the hundreds. The light and heat and dew and rain alternate, while the little bunches develop, mature, and take coloring. Now see our vine! How changed! Scarcely a leaf or a twig is visible. Nothing but fruit, covered over and gracefully pendent with clusters, wine-colored and luscious, while the sunbeams amid the clusters add a crimson richness and crystal transparency not to be described. You can read the picture.

How many hearts and households have been changed by these prunings! We are too full of the earth elements, growing lush and fat and unspiritual, putting out our arms for worldly good, grasping for things hurtful to our spiritual welfare. But he kindly took these away. We were twining the heart tendrils too closely about a loved one, giving it a place that God should have. He put in the pruning knife and cut the tendrils and left us to bleed in tears. But when the wounds were healed and the season of sorrow had passed, it found us subdued and changed and closer to God, the soul scarred, but better and richer and more fruitful.

It doesn't take much earth to support a vine. It will grow where scarcely anything else will. It requires but little soil. It will thrust out its rootlets and hunt sustenance in the fissures and crevices of the rocks and find life where other things would perish. It lives from the atmosphere and sunlight as much as, or more than, from the earth. It draws its life largely from the upper elements.

Like the vine, our religion will live anywhere and under any circumstances. It will grow up from poverty and grapple itself in amid adversity's rocks and flourish where there is little of this world to sustain it. Men say: "I must be in easy circumstances before I can be religious." When the truth is, easy circumstances are keeping more people from Christ and destroying more souls than poverty ever did or ever will. I may get too poor for some things, but never too poor for my religion to flourish. Lazarus in rags could grow in grace while living and have angel attendants to heaven when he died. We really need little of this world, but more of the heavenly atmosphere and the sunshine of grace. Let us labor to be fruitful in the things of God, for "Herein is my Father glorified, that ye bear much fruit."

THE ATONING BLOOD.

Text: "When I see the blood, I will pass over you." (Ex. xii. 13.)

"FOR the life of the flesh is in the blood." This statement stood for three thousand years before it caught the physiologist's notice. Draw out the blood, and you draw out the life. Close the wound in its own blood, and it heals by first intention. Nothing has such healing virtue as the blood. The eternal life of all flesh is in the blood of Christ. Out of his blood creation is created anew. Out of his blood are the issues of everlasting life.

Salvation is wholly of God. The bleeding Christ is the divine substitute for man, while there is no substitute for his blood. Substitution is the aim of the age, to eliminate the supernatural, get God out of the Scriptures, out of the literature, out of the experience of men, and account for all things on natural bases.

One preaches Christ as divine only in a limited

sense, another that the Scriptures are largely legendary and with hell relegated, the judgment seldom mentioned, Sinai silenced, repentance unnamed, and sinners coddled and sung to sleep with love ditties and soft lullabies, while the real gospel message is wellnigh an offense. The man who dares offer it is a back number and deserves to be retired.

But over all the word of God stood good in Egypt. He provided the lamb and required its blood over the door. Nothing more was required; nothing less would answer. A Hebrew might have substituted anything else and his first-born have died.

The Blood Neglected.

Yonder is the home of an eminent Hebrew who has neglected the blood; but his dwelling is of the true Israelitish style, with an altar on the housetop. Every environment tells, like the features of the Jewish face, that this is the home of a Hebrew. Then there is Moses himself standing sentry at the door and over the door in glowing letters shining out upon the darkness, "This is a Hebrew's home." Surely this home is safe, no danger here, when lo! the death messenger on dark and noiseless wings halts before that home and looks in vain for the blood. He bids Moses stand aside, and, passing into the home, the death gurgle is heard in the throat of the first-born, and the wail of grief goes up to an insulted God.

Nothing else will satisfy. Pious parentage, highest culture, most correct morals will not meet the demand. The outward life may be of the most approved Israelitish type, a man of renown in the Church, endowing universities, erecting hospitals, building homes for the helpless. God makes inquisition for none of these things. He maketh inquisition for blood. If the blood be not on the heart's doorway, we will perish under the death angel's hand.

Salvation is not by nice behavior in my way, but by the blood of Christ in God's way. I do this, and I don't do that. Do what we may or leave undone what we may, to ignore the blood is to be lost forever.

God demands its preëminence. It was not enough that the lamb was slain, but its blood must be over the door. Then the inmates would go neither in nor out without contact with that blood. "Out of the heart are the issues of life." Hence it is upon the heart that God requires the sprinkled blood. Then the thoughts, desires, and impulses which pass its doorway come in touch with the blood.

The blood in Egypt might have been set aside in a private place and the first-born in that home have perished. How many have a slain lamb set aside in their theory, a crucified Christ in their creed, while his blood is not upon their heart and life—Christ not visible in their character; God's requirement ignored and they exposed to destruction!

There is a legend of a Jewish girl who was ill and nigh unto death, who had a strange anxiety to know that the blood was upon the door. Her father assured her that he had given positive orders and that all was right. But she begged to be lifted from her couch and carried to the doorway that she might see the blood for herself. And lo! when they came the blood was not there. Be the legend true or not, it carries its lesson.

How many ungodly parents have been called to look for the blood through the influence of a dying child! It is not that men do not believe in the blood; they simply neglect and ignore it. It is in their creed and intention, but they wait until some sad providence calls them, like the father of the Jewish girl, to look and find that the blood is not upon their heart and life.

The angel saw nothing but the blood. He did not see the inmates. He knew not whether they were old or young, feeble or strong; but he saw the blood. They were sheltered behind it, and that was enough. Miserable hut though it was, with inmates on their beds of straw, yet they were allied to God, with his own blood seal over their doorway.

What a night! The first-born in every unprotected home must die. Nevertheless, the obedient Hebrew with the blood over his door gathers his dear ones within and sleeps as sweetly and safely as if there were no death angel abroad. O the sweet sense of safety under the blood!

God's Estimate.

This rests not on position, office, social prestige, or financial power. A man may be master of millions, make his corner on every commodity and upon the honest toil of his fellow men. A few such may buy up a republic and rob its myriads of their rights; but when they come before God face to face, their power will fall into paralysis. Even the gold standard will not answer at the judgment. It cannot make a corner on the atonement and put salvation into a trust. It is a blood standard there, and nothing else will pass.

Dives in diamonds is an offense, while Lazarus in rags is the object of divine favor; not because of his poverty, but because of his trust in the blood. The Pharisee before his altar in high self-esteem is an offense, while the wretched publican at the foot of the steps has God's pity and approval. And why? The one is thinking of himself, while the other smites himself and honors God. God will see nothing we can bring or boast; but he will see the blood. Nothing else will hide sin; but the blood will hide it. I say it reverently, God himself can see no sin in us when he looks through the blood. It removes all sin. Then let us walk through no day nor sleep through a night without the blood on the doorway of the heart.

This blood has a voice. In contemplating this blood the soul may well put off the shoes from its feet. It is holy ground. Its mystery laps back into the life of God before he had formed the earth and the world. It was in his thought then. He eternally intended to unite his life with the life of man. This precious blood was to ebb and flow in a human heart, even if there had been no sin, and the awful fact of the coming of sin could not change the divine intention.

Again, there is that strange property in human blood that it cannot be hid. Cain buried the first blood ever shed, but it cried unto God from the ground. Lady Macbeth could never wash its stain from her fair hands. Thousands have tried in vain to hide it. "Murder will out." Blood concealed still has a voice. It may be silent for decades; but some fortuity, some unguarded word, some guilty conscience on its deathbed will part the curtains and let the world see the bloody hand.

The blood of Christ has more than human voice. It speaks with more than "the tongues of men and of angels." You hear it in Holy Writ, from the opening promise to the closing Apocalypse, from Paradise to Patmos. It speaks through millions of Bibles to the ends of the earth. Ten thousand presses clap their great inky hands, printing out the pages that tell of this blood. We hear it in trumpet tones from ten thousand pulpits, while the lips of childhood's millions sing it in the Sunday schools of the land. The Holy Spirit also speaks of this precious blood in sacred silence to millions more. There is no speech nor language where its voice is not heard. God's eternal thought has become the world's universal anthem, and creation is vocal with the voice of that blood which cleanseth from all sin.

The Power of This Blood.

Jesus said: "If I be lifted up, if I bleed, I will draw all men unto me." The blood is the magnetic power of the gospel. The mob mocked him until he died, then returned smiting upon their breasts. This blood at Pentecost extorted the cry: "Men and brethren, what shall we do?" And three thousand were saved in a day. There was no substitute for the blood over the Hebrew door, and there is none for it in the pulpit to-day. It is the center and source of saving power. The pulpit is weak or strong in proportion to its nearness to the blood. A bloodless gospel is an emasculated gospel. God save the pulpit from the lullabies that soothe and keep men asleep in their sins! Better to have them awake swearing than not to awake them at all.

Its efficacy is absolute. It saves the worst and saves to the uttermost. Sufferers seek the world's Bethesdas only to meet disappointment, but the soul that comes to the fountain filled with blood is made every whit whole. There is no other Siloam. "I cannot wash my heart, but by believing thee and waiting for thy blood to impart the spotless purity."

The sight of the blood satisfies. His blood is the blood of peace. Since that awful tragedy the sun has not faltered nor the rocks rent. It gives peace on earth. Have I sinned, and is conscience warring against me? I fly to the blood and find peace and rest. Does Satan assail? I bring the blood, and the devil leaveth me. He turns from this blood with loathing, as an Egyptian would turn from the bloody Nile. Have I grieved the Holy Spirit? I bring the blood, and then he bears witness to my acceptance. Is God angry because of my sins? I fly to the blood and hear him say: "When I see the blood I will pass over you." Am I dying? Let me breathe my life out under the blood. Have I come to the gate of the eternal city? The sentry asks not my name, denomination, or nationality; but he sees the blood and bids me enter into the joys of my Lord.

This blood is God's ultimatum. It is omnipotence *in extremis*, the pouring out of God's life. He can do no more than utter the tragic ultimatum: "It is finished!"

The world had caught glimpses of divine love in the soft sunlight, had heard it in the Æolian winds, in the breathing of the flowers, and in the low music of the gentle rain; but they had seen only the surface of the love sea. There was a sea beneath the sea, a sea unseen and unthought. It was the gulf stream of this nether sea that broke upon the world in the tragedy of Calvary and showed the heart of God to men. It took God's life to tell his love. Here is love in divine exhaustion. Behold this blood and know the doom of him who slights or disregards it.

The Unpardonable Sin.

What is it? It is the disregard of the atoning blood. Abuse one of God's mercies, and he has a million more. Break all the commandments, and when the law springs its merciless guillotine for your execution you may fly to this blood and escape the stroke. But slight the blood, count it a thing of naught, and there remaineth no more sacrifice for sin. God himself cannot help you then. He can do no more. Logically, then, is your sin unpardonable. There is no other remedy. Here, then, is humanity's only hope. Out of this blood are the issues of life. The life eternal of all flesh is in this blood. Come under its crimson cover this good hour. Let the saint see that the blood is over his doorway. Let the sinner fly to this refuge. Escape for thy life. God hath spoken and will keep his word: "When I see the blood, I will pass over you."

The Pale Horse and His Rider.

Text: "And I looked, and behold, a pale horse: and his name that sat on him was Death, and Hell followed with him." (Rev. vi. 8.)

WE have here a thrilling picture of the great conqueror of conquerors. The monarch is mounted and moving. The horse indicates speed, a speed from which none may escape; his pale color is significant of his mission. The magnitude of his conquests is seen in his following. Hell, or Hades, followed with him, the receptacle of departed spirits, with its countless millions as his escort.

He finds his victims everywhere. He takes his captives from every home and at all times, at sunny noon and solemn night. We have heard and will hear again the relentless hoofs of the pale horse until one by one the loved ones are all in his captivity. His conquests will increase until time shall be no more, until a mightier than he shall command his surrender. Death shall then dismount, his captive millions be liberated, and death and Hades shall give up their dead. The pale horse and rider shall perish, and there shall be no more death.

The Nature of Death.

Since death is real and we, with our families, are to meet it, how important that we should have all the knowledge of it possible! What is death? and what is its effect upon us? Death is a change, solemn, absolute, complete. The natural functions and forces cease, the gates of the senses all close simultaneously, and the curtain falls. The tableaux of time dissolve and pass from sight. Death ends the old relations and surrounds us with new ones; the eyes close on earthly scenes, the ears die to earthly sounds, and the hands are folded from earthly toil.

Disembodied, we step upon a new shore, where life is upon new principles. It is a second conversion. "Old things pass away, and all things become new." Death is not more wonderful than life; it is only another change added to the changes through which we are ever passing; only this is the last. It closes a sort of embryo being in which we see darkly and introduces us into an enlarged and elevated state, where we shall "know perfectly what we now know in part."

Your birth was your first change, and that gave you consciousness; the nursery your first world, from which you gradually took in a world that was higher; and now in your maturity the spinning-top and hobby-horse days are like a long-past dream. The difference between that world and your world of to-day is what life has done. If life has wrought such wonders with us, is it any more wonderful that death should bring great changes? To die is but to pass into a higher and clearer life.

The unhatched birdling is in the midst of the scenes of its future being. It is not distance that shuts out the air and the sunlight; it is only the thin shell, and the breaking of this crystal is not a change of place, but of conditions.

Thus while living we are as much in eternity as we will ever be. Eternity surrounds us now, and supernatural things press about us, and we often catch glimpses of them. It is not distance, but it is this shell of clay that hides from us the sunlight of eternity. Death will break this chrysalis of clay and open the door to the imprisoned spirit. It is death that brings the supernatural into view. May it not be that when death unbars the door and the loved one comes into newborn liberty it may linger in the room to look on while we weep and wring the hands and, were it possible, would gladly comfort us in our grief?

Death the Great Specialist.

We often carry the suffering loved one a long way to have some specialist treat his malady. Death is the great specialist whose practice is as old as time and as wide as the world. He comes without summons when all other physicians and remedies have failed, and his touch gives rest and sleep, like the affrighted babe among strangers whose cry is incessant and whose anguish is untold until the mother comes, then on her bosom it sobs itself to sleep and forgets its distress. Thus hurting humanity, with agonies too grievous to be borne, when past human aid or comfort, when the death angel comes, then on its bosom the groans cease, and they forget their anguish and sweetly sleep.

There is somewhere a picture of a frightful face, livid and ghastly, from which one would turn away with horror but for a hideous fascination which draws one toward it. But on approaching, the fearful face is changed into the face of an angel. It is a picture of death.

Walk over the battle field after the conflict. The smoke has gathered into a cloud above; horses and men mangled, groaning, and bleeding in helplessness;

men begging for water and praying for mercy; while the brutes by piteous moans tell out in their own way of what they suffer; and that peculiar and sickening odor common to the battle field adds faintness to the horrors. Surgeons cut and bind, chaplains pray and seek to comfort, but no mortal ministry can bring relief to hundreds of the fallen; yet when the death angel passes silently over the scene the groans are hushed, the blood stanched, the pains cease, and the sufferers sleep as sweetly as the loved ones they have left in the old churchyard.

Death never brings an added pain, but relieves the pain already too grievous to be borne. Think of a world groaning and travailing in pain and of the relief that death has brought to the hopeless millions, then tell us if his is not a mission of mercy.

Death comes only in hopeless cases. He does not intrude when the trouble is slight and only temporary, but comes only when disease has proved too much for skill and remedies. But when the sufferer is given up to suffer forever unless some deliverer comes, then death comes to the rescue. Death is king over all diseases. Like the eagle king, ever on watch for the fishhawk's prey, the death angel, mightier than all diseases, is ever on watch for the sufferer hopeless of recovery. Sometimes we long for his coming. When the loved one has passed beyond the possibility of recovery, and every hour and moment are only anguish, to think of their remaining in that state forever, doomed to suffer thus perpetually, is too awful to contemplate. Yet this would be the doom of every hopeless sufferer but for the kindly ministry of death.

Hence, after all our dread of death and fighting against it, it is our best friend, next to Him who is Conqueror of death.

Eliminate every disease from the catalogue, and what would the world be without death? Time would soon lay on the couch of helpless age, to become a ceaseless burden upon others; our fathers, grandfathers, and the previous generations as helpless babes on our hands; the world a nursery of babes a thousand years old; while we would be worn with the crushing and ever-increasing care. How the world would cry in anguish for the return of death! Next to the blood of Christ, this poor world needs the ministries of death.

The Realization of Death.

In this we cannot have the benefit of experience, our own or that of others. Others can help us by giving us their experience in every form of suffering; but none have ever given us their experience in death. We have reason to believe that when disembodied our powers of perception will be increased. "Sown in weakness, raised in power." God is without body or physical parts; yet he perceives in a higher and broader sense than is possible to us. Hence when we are like him, free from cumbrous mortality, we shall perceive in a higher and more perfect sense than now.

You have felt the exhilaration of the balmy air of a bright spring day when carried into it from the sick room. I remember when, after confinement for five long months, I was carried for the first time into the open air. It was a revelation, a new life, and like paradise to my spirit. What, then, must be that transition from the sick room into the paradise of God? The restful tranquillity of that home which he is preparing for faithful children who suffer here.

The Expectation of Death.

When the mind is wound up and set for some important event, some unusual trial which has taken up our thought and solicitude, when it has come and gone, then we have a strange reverse of feeling. So when death has come and gone and with it all lassitude, dullness, and disappointment, then will come the happy, heavenly realization of the disembodied spirit, as if it said to itself: "So now all is over. This is what I have looked and waited for. I spent life getting ready for this—fasting, praying, working, and trusting—and now it is over. How light it seemed at last! I had anticipated it, and when I came to it I found it was only the shadow of death. Christ had taken the substance away. Now I am beyond death, have crossed the strange, dark river, and am in the land which has been in mind on all the life journey." Then will come the sweet, strange reverse of feeling that comes with the first experience of disembodied being.

> "O harmless death, whom still the valiant brave,
> The wise expect, the sorrowful invite,
> And all the good embrace who know the grave
> A short, dark passage to eternal light!"

www.ingramcontent.com/pod-product-compliance
Lightning Source LLC
Chambersburg PA
CBHW022354040426
42450CB00005B/183